LOWFAT AMERICAN FAVORITES

Goldie Silverman and Jacqueline B. Williams

A Nitty Gritty® Cookbook

©1990 Bristol Publishing Enterprises, Inc. P.O. Box 1737, San Leandro, California 94577. World rights reserved. No part of this publication may be reproduced by any mechanical, photographic, or electronic process, or in the form of a phonographic recording, nor may it be stored in a retrieval system, transmitted, or otherwise copied for public or private use without prior written permission from the publisher.

Printed in the United States of America.

ISBN 0-911954-95-3

Cover photography: Kathryn Opp
Food stylist: Carol Cooper Ladd
Cover graphics: Vicki L. Crampton
Illustrator: Carol Webb Atherly

Table of Contents

Goldie Silverman and Jackie Williams have done it again! They have created a cookbook of American foods that fit right into today's life style. The recipes meet dietary guidelines for lowering fat and cholesterol while using wholesome foods naturally high in dietary fiber. Salt and sugar are used sparingly. No guess work is needed here—each tasty recipe is accompanied with its nutrient composition so you can choose what you need easily.

Evette M. Hackman, R.D., Ph.D.
Private practice, Edmonds, Washington
Nutrition and food writer for ***Shape, American Health, Northwest Runner*** and ***The Everett Herald***

Introduction

The Surgeon General of the United States stated in 1988 that all Americans should limit the amount of fats, *especially saturated fats*, that they eat.

The prestigious National Research Council, which draws on the work of the most noted scientists in the country, came out with a report in 1989 called *Diet and Health: Implications for Reducing Chronic Disease Risk*, which listed nine recommendations for preventive health care. The first one was to reduce consumption of saturated fats.*

In magazines, newspapers and television, and in our doctor's offices, we are admonished to get our blood cholesterol down to an acceptable level. We should accomplish this feat, we are told, by eating the right foods and by avoiding foods high in saturated fat and cholesterol.

The twelve most popular main dishes in the United States, according to *The Book of Lists* (David Wallechinsky et al.), are fried chicken, roast beef, spag-

* See Appendix, page 149, for summary of National Research Council report.

hetti, turkey, baked ham, fried shrimp, beef stew, meat loaf, fish, macaroni and cheese, pot roast and Swiss steak. Many of these entrees are high in saturated fat and cholesterol.

Here is the problem all of us face, the problem that this book will help you solve: to reduce the total amount of fat and especially saturated fat in our daily diets while at the same time continuing to eat the foods that are our favorites.

Impossible? No. Difficult? Not necessarily. In this book, we will show you that you can cut down on the amount of fat that you eat every day and still enjoy tasty, familiar and satisfying menus. We will give you techniques that you can apply to your own family's favorite dishes.

First, it helps to know a little bit about dietary fats, what they are and what they do.

Fats in the Blood Stream

Think of your blood stream as a complicated river system, picking up products in one part of your body and delivering them to another. Some of these products are the foods that you have eaten (broken down into chemical compounds), and some are products manufactured in your body from the foods that you have consumed. Some products are both!

When you have a physical examination, a small amount of blood is withdrawn and sent to a laboratory for analysis; many of the products in the blood are examined, but the ones we are most concerned with here are the *lipids* (fats) which include cholesterol. If your doctor tells you your blood cholesterol level or your LDL or HDL numbers show that you are at risk, you should immediately begin to make the dietary changes that may help improve the numbers.

Cholesterol is one product that is both manufactured in our bodies and consumed in foods. Cholesterol is a waxy component of fat that the body uses to make hormones; however, excess cholesterol can be deposited on the inner lining of arteries where it reduces and finally stops the flow of blood. All animals, including humans, make cholesterol in their livers, so when a doctor tells us that our blood cholesterol level is high, some of that cholesterol is our own and some comes from the saturated fats we have eaten: butter, cheese, milk, meats, lard, coconut oil and palm oil.

The other *lipids* that are a factor in fatty deposits in blood vessels are high-density lipoproteins (HDL), sometimes called "good lipids," and low-density lipoproteins (LDL), the "bad" ones; your doctor is the best person to interpret the numbers for you.

Even if you're getting good lab reports, too much fat is not a good thing. Fat that isn't deposited in the arteries is stored by the body for future use, and fat that isn't used leads to obesity. Obesity, in turn, seems to increase the likelihood of many diseases, including diabetes and some cancers, as well as heart disease.

Dietary Goals

Many thinking people have come to the conclusion that they can prolong their lives and increase their health by paying more attention to the foods that they eat. When we wrote our first cookbook, ***No Salt, No Sugar, No Fat***, and our second, we said that fat, salt and sugar were the "three villains" of the American diet. (Sugar is bad when it keeps bad company; it is too often found with butter, cream and cream cheese.) By our third book we had added the villain cholesterol.

In this, our fourth book, we're listing another villain: *saturated fat*. The United States Department of Agriculture's Human Nutrition Information Service has stated: "*Eating extra saturated fat, excess calories and high levels of cholesterol will increase blood cholesterol in many people.*" In other words, a diet high in saturated fat may tend to raise the blood cholesterol level, which in turn increases fatty deposits on blood vessel walls. Some researchers say that limiting the amount of saturated fat that we eat is just as important as limiting the cholesterol.

Saturated fat in the American diet comes from two main sources: fat from meat, dairy products, lard and hydrogenated shortenings; and fat from the so-called "tropical" group, including coconut oil, palm and palm kernel oils and cocoa butter.

Nutritional Information

Nutritional information per serving x calories, x% calories from fat, x grams fat (x tsp. fat), x grams saturated fat, x mg. cholesterol, x grams protein, x grams carbohydrate, x mg sodium

Each recipe in this book includes nutritional information per serving, just like the one above, to help you figure the amounts of calories, fats and other food components that you eat every meal and every day. Our nutritional information comes from a computer program called ***"The Food Processor II, Nutrition and Diet Analysis System"**** which is based on USDA data plus 330 other sources; where it was appropriate, we also consulted food product manufacturers. The analyses of meats were based on foods that were already cooked, so you should weigh and measure after cooking; other foods were analyzed

* ESHA Research, P.O. Box 13028, Salem, OR 97309

before cooking. If an alternative ingredient is listed, the nutritional information is given for the first ingredient mentioned. If this nutritional information is going to be meaningful to you, you *must* follow our serving sizes given at the top of each recipe. If you eat more than a serving, multiply the nutritional information numbers by the number of servings you eat!

For this book, we have set some daily dietary goals to help our readers plan their meals, goals that follow the guidelines of the USDA and those of the National Institutes of Health and of the American Heart Association.

The total amount of *all* fats consumed in one day should be no more than 30% of total calories. That percentage includes all fats, both the kind used in cooking or spread on bread and the kind that naturally occurs in meat, dairy products and other foods. Even if most of the fats you eat are "good" fats, the total amount should not exceed 30%. Saturated fats (which are included in the total) should by themselves be no more than 10%. You can figure the percentage of calories from fat if you remember that a gram of fat is 9 calories. So if the label says that a serving of prepared food is 100 calories with 10 grams of fat, you can figure 90 calories or 90% are from fat. The nutritional information that we have provided with each recipe has done that figuring for you.

We've included a chart to help you find the daily levels of fats you should aim for, according to the amounts of calories you normally consume.

Daily Levels of Fat Consumption

Calories	Calories from fat	Grams fat	Grams saturated fat
1500	450	50	17
1800	540	60	20
2100	630	70	23

This chart shows that a person who eats 1800 calories per day should consume no more than 540 of those calories from fat, or about 60 grams of fat; of these, only 20 grams should be saturated fat. Dividing these numbers by three meals per day, we concluded that each meal should contain no more than 20 grams of total fat, and no more than 6.5 grams of saturated fat.

Cholesterol levels should be kept to no more than 300 mg. per day.

Although salt is not listed as a bad guy in the title to this book, we still believe, with the surgeon general, that Americans consume too much sodium (a component of salt). healthy individuals should keep their daily sodium intake to 2000-3000 mg. For this cookbook, which is about avoiding fat, we prepared recipes made with regular ingredients, so even though we use no salt in our recipes, the sodium levels might seem high for a person on a low-sodium diet. When we cook for our own families, we avoid ingredients that are high in sodium, substitute lots of other seasonings for salt, and choose the low-salt or salt-free version of tomato products, canned vegetables and other foods. We recommend to that our readers choose low-salt or low-sodium ingredients.

Our Favorite Techniques

If you have made the decision to cut down on the fat and salt in your diet, you don't have to discard the entire collection of recipes you have been assembling for years, but you do need to substitute some new techniques for the old and develop a new awareness of what you are eating. Don't try to make every change overnight. Give yourself time; make a schedule for gradually reducing the fat in your diet. We like to say, "Begin with cutting down, and lead to cutting out."

Cutting Down on Fat

Reduce by one-half the amount of fat in your old recipes. After 6 weeks, reduce fat to one-fourth the original amount. Work toward making your recipes fat-free.

Limit the total amount of meat, fish and poultry that you eat in one day to no more than 6 ounces (cooked). The American Heart Association suggests that you limit the amount of additional fat that you eat in one day from all other sources (spreads on bread, dressings on salads, fats in cooking) to no more than 5 to 8 teaspoonsful of fat (20 to 32 grams).

Trim all visible fat from meat before you cook it. Remove the skin as well as the fat from chicken. Choose fish and chicken more often than red meat.

Substitute fillets of turkey breast for veal or pork cutlets. Use turkey ham instead of the old-fashioned kind. Choose lean cuts of beef or pork, cuts that show no white marbling. Cook on a rack whenever possible. Avoid bacon and sausages, unless they are lowfat turkey sausages.

Pour pan juices into a fat separator; wait for the fat to rise and carefully pour off juices, leaving the fat behind. Or pour pan juices into a glass jar, wait, and discard the fat, leaving the good juices behind.

Reduce the amount of cheese that you eat, and limit your cheeses to those that contain no more than 5 grams of fat per ounce. (Kraft makes reduced fat cheeses called Kraft Light.)

Adapt your recipes that use a white sauce made of butter, flour and milk. Instead, use 1 tbs. cornstarch to thicken 1 cup of nonfat milk; dissolve the cornstarch in cold milk and heat, stirring, until thick. Or slowly add 1 cup water or stock to a mixture of ½ cup instant nonfat dry milk powder, 1 tbs. flour, and 1 tbs. cornstarch; cook and stir until thick.

When the recipe says, "brown meat in fat," you can brown with just 1/4 tsp. oil in a nonstick skillet, or with no fat at all on a rack under the broiler. Transfer browned meat onto paper towels to absorb fat, wipe out the skillet (if you're going to continue using it), and then proceed with your recipe. If your meat is fatty, don't flour it before browning; that just seals in the fat. Add flour later if you want it for thickening.

Cook stews, soups and spaghetti sauces a day ahead and refrigerate them. Remove the fat that solidifies on top before reheating them.

Change the ratio of oil to vinegar in salad dressings. Some high quality, high acidic (6-7%) vinegars are actually less harsh than some of lower acidity (4%). Try some specialty vinegars, like raspberry or sherry vinegars. Work toward equal parts oil and vinegar.

Switch to reduced calorie mayonnaise. Stop using butter; choose other spreads, like jam or preserves, for your breakfast toast and mustard for sandwiches.

Cutting Down on Saturated Fats

Substitute the "good" fats—those that are polyunsaturated or monounsaturated—for "bad" saturated fats. The best oils are low erucic-acid rapeseed (Canola), safflower, olive and corn oils; the worst are animal fats, including butter, and the "tropical" oils—coconut, palm or palm kernel oils and cocoa butter. Canola and safflower oils are interchangeable in our recipes. Where we use olive oil, we chose it for its distinctive flavor; it should not be substituted in other dishes unless you want the olive taste.

Read labels carefully. Use margarine that lists as its first ingredient either liquid corn oil, safflower oil or rapeseed oil; avoid margarines made with palm oil or coconut oil and spreads that are part butter. Don't buy crackers, cookies or cereals made with animal fats or with the tropical oils.

Choose dairy products that are nonfat or lowfat. Drink nonfat (skim) milk and eat nonfat yogurt and cottage cheese. Use lowfat ricotta cheese instead of cream cheese. Don't be misled; lowfat ricotta is lower in fat than skim milk ricotta.

Extend the flavor of cheese by combining a small amount of strong-tasting cheese, like Roquefort, with a larger quantity of lowfat ricotta or lowfat cottage cheese.

Limit the total amount of all fats that you eat, even if all of them are "good" fats, just as you limit the total amount of foods that you eat to keep your weight in control. Eventually, your body will turn all excess foods into stored fat, and that will contribute to all the problems associated with obesity.

Cutting Down on Cholesterol

The egg is probably the greatest source of cholesterol in the American diet; that is, the egg *yolk* is the greatest source. One egg yolk contains 210 mg. of cholesterol, while the whites contain hardly any fat at all! So it you cut out just the yolks, you can continue to use many of your old recipes. Replace 1 whole egg with 2 egg whites, or use 1 egg white plus 1 tsp. safflower oil for 1 egg. Sometimes you can use 1 whole egg plus 2 egg whites for 2 whole eggs.

Egg substitutes are another way to cut down on cholesterol. Egg substitutes, sometimes called "imitation eggs," are products found in the frozen food section (for example, Egg Beaters brand) or in the dairy section (Second Nature brand). Use egg substitutes whenever your recipe calls for eggs that don't have to be separated.

Are deviled eggs your specialty? Hard-cook eggs in the usual way, discard the yolks, and stuff the halves with lowfat ricotta or cottage cheese or with pureed tofu (soy bean curd) that has been combined with your customary seasoning. A little mustard, curry powder or turmeric will add yellow color.

Most people who are placed on lowfat or cholesterol-lowering diets are still allowed 2 or 3 eggs per week. You can choose to use your eggs in baking or in egg-rich noodles, but if you eat 1/4 of a yolk here and another 1/2 a yolk there, you may find at the end of the week that you've eaten 5 or 6 eggs instead of the 2 you were allotted. We prefer to eat our 2 eggs as recognizable eggs; we like a whole poached egg on a toasted English muffin once a week for breakfast, or half of a hard-cooked egg on a chef salad. When the eggs are hidden, as in baking, we don't need the real things.

Reading Labels

Don't wait until you're facing the stove, ready to cook, to make nutritional decisions. Awareness of what you are eating begins in the supermarket, when you buy your foods. Learn to read labels. Carry a magnifying glass if the print is too small.

Remember that ingredients on a label are listed according to the quantity of each; there is more of the first ingredient than of the second, more of the second than the third, and so on.

Look for the kind of fats in a product; reject products with animal or tropical fats. Figure out the percentage of calories per serving from fat; remember that 1 gram of fat is always 9 calories.

Consider the serving size; a product may seem to be lowfat, but if the serving size listed is only 1/4 the quantity you know you'll eat, you have to multiply all the numbers by 4.

Cutting Down on Salt

Gradually adjust to less salt just as you work toward using less fat. Halve the amount of salt in your standard recipes, and substitute a salt-free seasoning mix instead. There are many different brands on the market; experiment until you find two or three that you like. We find that we like a blend with lots of parsley and herbs to use on salads and a different blend with intriguing Middle Eastern spices for meats. For the table, refill your salt shakers with a variety of salt-free mixes.

Use onion or garlic powder instead of onion or garlic salt. Use a half teaspoon of vinegar or lemon juice, or a whole clove of garlic, to season the cooking water for rice or noodles. Experiment with herbs and spices; begin with 1/4 teaspoon dry herbs, and play around with different combinations.

Breakfast and Brunch

What do you eat for breakfast, now that you're not eating eggs and meat? Remember that it's the egg yolk that's the cholesterol-loaded bad guy. Many of the familiar foods that you're used to eating, like pancakes and muffins, can still be prepared with just the egg white or with imitation egg products.

Toast, muffins, breads and pancakes don't need butter. Enhance them instead with good jams and preserves, lowfat ricotta cheese, nonfat yogurt and fresh fruit.

Cereals, hot and cold, are other traditional favorites. Instead of loading them up with heavy cream and sugar, eat them with fresh fruit and nonfat milk or yogurt.

Brunch Bread

16 slices

A daughter-in-law brought us an old cookbook handed down in her family. In it we found this dense bread. Try it spread with lowfat ricotta cheese.

1½ cups nonfat milk
1 tbs. vinegar or lemon juice
1½ cups all-purpose flour
1 tsp. baking powder
1 tsp. soda
½ cup brown sugar
¾ cup Nabisco 100% Bran cereal
¾ cup rolled oats
½ cup raisins
½ cup finely chopped walnuts

Preheat oven to 375°. Line a 9" loaf pan with waxed paper. In a small bowl, combine milk with vinegar and set aside 2 to 3 minutes to sour. In a large bowl, mix flour, baking powder, soda, sugar and cereals. Stir in soured milk; add raisins and nuts. Pour into pan and bake 45 minutes to 1 hour. Bread is done when a toothpick inserted into center comes out clean. Cool in pan 10 minutes. Finish cooling on a wire rack.

Nutritional information per slice 139 calories, 18% calories from fat, 3 grams fat (¾ tsp. fat), 0 grams saturated fat, 0 mg cholesterol, 4 grams protein, 26 grams carbohydrate, 109 mg sodium

Cranberry Bread

10 slices

Long before Ocean Spray popularized cranberry sauce, Native Americans were combining this mouth-puckering berry with wild honey.

1 cup all-purpose flour
¾ cup whole wheat flour
2 tsp. baking powder
½ tsp. baking soda
2 egg whites or imitation egg equal to 1 egg
2 tbs. safflower oil
¼ cup sugar
¼ cup nonfat dry milk powder
¾ cup orange or blended fruit juice
1½ cups cranberries, chopped
¼ cup walnuts, chopped
¼ cup raisins

Preheat oven to 350°. In a large bowl, sift together flours, baking powder and soda. In another bowl, beat together egg whites, oil, sugar, dry milk and juices. Pour into dry ingredients and mix just until blended. Stir in cranberries, walnuts and raisins. Pour batter into a lightly greased nonstick loaf pan (4½"x8½") and let stand 10 minutes before baking. Bake for 50 minutes or until a toothpick inserted into center comes out clean.

Nutritional information per slice 174 calories, 25% calories from fat, 5 grams fat (1¼ tsp. fat), .5 grams saturated fat, .3 mg cholesterol, 5 grams protein, 29 grams carbohydrate, 128 mg sodium

Zucchini-Date Bread

10 slices

Toasted and spread with lowfat ricotta cheese and good preserves, this wonderful bread makes breakfast a special treat.

¾ cup all-purpose flour
1 tsp. baking powder
½ tsp. baking soda
1 tsp. cinnamon
½ tsp. nutmeg
1 cup oat bran
4 egg whites or imitation egg equal to 2 eggs
½ cup sugar
¼ cup safflower oil
¼ cup orange juice
1 cup grated zucchini
½ cup chopped dates

Preheat oven to 350°. In a small bowl, sift together flour, baking powder, baking soda and seasonings; stir in oat bran and set aside. In a large bowl, beat together egg whites, sugar, oil and orange juice; add zucchini and dates. Stir flour into egg-zucchini mixture and mix until just blended. Pour batter into a lightly greased nonstick loaf pan (4½"x8½"); bake for 50 to 55 minutes. Cool in pan 5 minutes and finish cooling on a wire rack.

Nutritional information per slice 179 calories, 28% calories from fat, 6 grams fat (1½ tsp. fat), .6 grams saturated fat, 0 mg cholesterol, 4 grams protein, 32 grams carbohydrate, 81 mg sodium

Blueberry Whole Wheat Muffins

12 muffins

Whole wheat muffins will not be cakelike, but whole wheat flour has a wonderful nutty quality. If you are just beginning to use whole wheat grains, try half whole wheat and half white flour, or look for whole wheat pastry flour.

3 egg whites or imitation egg equal to 2 eggs
2 tbs. safflower or corn oil
2 tbs. honey or blueberry jam
1 cup apple juice or cider
2 cups whole wheat flour
1/2 cup white flour
2 tsp. baking powder
1 cup fresh or frozen blueberries

Preheat oven to 400°. In a large mixing bowl, beat together egg whites, oil, honey and juice; set aside. In another bowl, combine flours and baking powder. Add dry ingredients to liquid, stirring only until moistened. Allow batter to stand 5 minutes. Stir in blueberries. Pour batter into a lightly greased or paper-lined muffin pan. Bake for 20 to 25 minutes.

Nutritional information per muffin 128 calories, 19% calories from fat, 3 grams fat (3/4 tsp. fat), .2 grams saturated fat, 0 mg cholesterol, 4 grams protein, 23 grams carbohydrate, 69 mg sodium

Applesauce Pancakes

16 (3") pancakes

Top these with blueberry sauce for a special treat.

1 cup whole wheat flour
1/4 cup oat bran
2 tbs. brown sugar
1 tbs. baking powder
1 tsp. cinnamon
3 egg whites or imitation eggs equal to 2 eggs
1 tbs. safflower oil
1 cup nonfat milk
1 cup applesauce, no sugar added
1/4 cup raisins, optional

In a large mixing bowl, combine dry ingredients. In another bowl, beat together egg whites, oil, milk and applesauce; pour over dry ingredients. Add raisins and stir until just blended. Cook on a lightly greased nonstick griddle or skillet until both sides are golden.

Nutritional information per pancake 59 calories, 16% calories from fat, 1 gram fat (1/4 tsp. fat), .1 gram saturated fat, .3 mg cholesterol, 2 grams protein, 11 grams carbohydrate, 81 mg sodium

Fruited French Toast

Servings: 6

We freeze pitted sweet cherries, Italian prune halves, peach slices or blueberries in 1-quart plastic containers. On Saturday night we take a box out of the freezer, and it's all thawed and ready for this brunch dish Sunday morning.

1 qt. frozen fruit, thawed
3 tbs. sugar
1/2 tsp. ground cinnamon
4 egg whites or imitation eggs equal to 3 eggs
½ cup nonfat milk
6 slices stale bread

Preheat oven to 400°. Arrange fruit in an 11"x17" baking dish. Combine sugar and cinnamon; sprinkle half over fruit. In a bowl, combine remaining sugar and cinnamon mixture, egg whites and milk; beat well. Dip bread slices in egg mixture to coat both sides. Arrange bread over fruit so that fruit is completely covered. Pour any remaining egg over bread. Bake for 20 to 25 minutes until bread is golden brown.

Nutritional information per serving 279 calories, 6% calories from fat, 2 grams fat (½ tsp. fat), 0 grams saturated fat, 1 mg cholesterol, 8 grams protein, 60 grams carbohydrate, 164 mg sodium

Cheese Puff

Servings: 4

Prepare this brunch dish on Saturday night for a hassle-free Sunday morning.

8 slices day-old bread
4 ozs. reduced fat sharp cheese (under 5 grams fat per oz.)
2 cups nonfat milk
3 egg whites plus 1 whole egg or imitation eggs equal to 3 eggs
1/2 tsp. dry mustard
1/2 tsp. paprika

Trim 4 slices of bread to fit the bottom of a shallow 8" casserole. Slice cheese and scatter evenly over bread. Arrange remaining bread on top of cheese. In a medium bowl, mix milk, imitation eggs and seasoning, and pour over bread and cheese. Cover with plastic wrap and refrigerate overnight or for at least 3 hours. Bake for 1 hour in a preheated 350° oven.

Variation

Substitute a mild (Swiss or Monterey Jack) reduced fat cheese, omit mustard and paprika, and season with 1/2 tsp. freshly grated nutmeg. Serve with raspberry or currant jam.

Nutritional information per serving 285 calories, 27% calories from fat, 8 grams fat (2 tsp. fat), 4 grams saturated fat, 23 mg cholesterol, 21 grams protein, 31 grams carbohydrate, 489 mg sodium

Blueberry Dumplings

Servings: 6

Imagine this breakfast cooked over a camp stove with really fresh wild blueberries! Combine the dry ingredients in a plastic bag. Carry dry milk to reconstitute in camp, and mix all in the bag.

1 pint fresh blueberries
1 cup water
1/4 cup sugar or honey
1 tbs. lemon juice
1 cup all-purpose flour
1 tbs. sugar
2 tsp. baking powder
1 tsp. finely grated lemon peel or zest
1 tbs. polyunsaturated margarine
1/2 cup nonfat milk

In a medium saucepan, combine berries, water and sugar. Cover, bring to a boil, reduce heat and simmer for 5 minutes. Add lemon juice. In a medium bowl, sift together flour, sugar and baking powder. Cut in lemon peel and margarine until it looks like cornmeal. Add milk all at once and stir until all flour is moistened. Drop batter in 6 equal portions onto bubbling blueberries; do not overlap dumplings. Cover tightly; cook over low heat for 10 minutes. Serve hot.

Nutritional information per serving 170 calories, 12% calories from fat, 2 grams fat (1/2 tsp. fat), 0 grams saturated fat, 0 mg cholesterol, 3 grams protein, 35 grams carbohydrate, 140 mg sodium

Rum and Cider Baked Apples

Servings: 4

In Washington state where apples reign as king, this is a favorite at brunch before a football game.

2 tbs. raisins or dried currants
4 tbs. dark rum
4 baking apples (MacIntosh, Winesap, Rome or Golden Delicious)
2 tbs. chopped dates
2 tbs. slivered almonds or crunchy cereal
1 tbs. brown sugar
½ tsp. cinnamon
½ tsp. freshly grated nutmeg
1 cup apple cider

Preheat oven to 375°. Soak raisins in rum for 30 minutes; drain and save rum. Wash and core apples. In a medium bowl, combine raisins with remaining ingredients, except cider, and stuff apples. Place apples in a baking dish. Combine cider and rum; spoon over apples. Bake until apples are tender, about 45 minutes.

Nutritional information per serving 253 calories, 12% calories from fat, 3 grams fat (¾ tsp. fat), .4 grams saturated fat, 0 mg cholesterol, 2 grams protein, 51 grams carbohydrate, 6 mg sodium

Fruit Compote

Servings: 8

We like to serve this with lowfat ricotta cheese that has been sweetened with apple juice.

4 apples, chopped, or 2 pears and 2 apples
½ cup dried figs or prunes, chopped
½ cup raisins
⅔ cup apple juice
juice of ½ lemon
1 cinnamon stick
2 oranges, peeled, seeded, sliced
1 cup seedless grapes

In a medium saucepan, combine apples, dried fruit, juices and cinnamon. Bring to a boil, cover and simmer 30 minutes. Mix in oranges and grapes; simmer for 15 minutes. Serve warm or cool.

Nutritional information per serving 167 calories, 4% calories from fat, .8 grams fat (⅛ tsp. fat), .1 gram saturated fat, 0 mg cholesterol, 1 gram protein, 43 grams carbohydrate, 5 mg sodium

Fresh Fruit Breakfast Drink

Servings: 1

Kerry, who gave us this drink, chooses strawberries or peaches as her fruit in summer, and apple chunks or kiwi in winter. She says it is important to use fresh fruit, but we have tried 1/4 cup frozen juice concentrate as the "fruit," and we think it's just fine.

1 cup nonfat buttermilk
1 banana
1 cup fresh fruit of your choice, cut into chunks
2 tbs. oat bran

Combine all ingredients in a blender or food processor and process until thick and smooth. Serve immediately.

Nutritional information per serving 292 calories, 6% calories from fat, 2 grams fat (1/2 tsp. fat), .8 grams saturated fat, 5 mg cholesterol, 12 grams protein, 67 grams carbohydrate, 215 mg sodium

Salads

Salad would seem to be a good choice for the person looking to reduce the fat in his or her diet, but unless the ingredients are chosen carefully, a salad may be the source of hidden fats. Today, when almost every supermarket and fast food outlet has a salad bar where you find crisp fresh vegetables and fruit, as well as prepared salads, marinated salads, a choice of toppings and a variety of dressings, it's more important than ever to be selective. A large quantity of meats, cheeses, croutons or seeds can raise the fat, and thus the calories, of an otherwise healthy salad. Dressings too should be examined with a suspicious eye for fat content.

The same thing is true for the salads you make at home. Replace the high-fat ingredients in your salads with cooked chicken or fish or reduced fat cheeses. Look for new combinations of vegetables to add to the basic lettuce and tomato salad; raw or cooked broccoli, cauliflower, green or wax beans, frozen peas or corn all add texture, color and surprising flavors. Fruits have a place in vegetable salads too; sliced oranges, apples, pears and grapes all work well. Cooked grains will give your salads crunch.

You will notice that our creamy salad dressings are made with reduced calorie mayonnaise and nonfat yogurt. The proportion of oil to vinegar in our vinaigrettes has been reduced to 1:1; if the dressing seems too tart for you, add a bit of honey or sugar. You can adapt your favorite dressings in the same way, or you can buy prepared dressings that are low in fat.

With salads, as with every other food, portion size is important. If you eat more than one serving, you must figure all of the fat that you eat in your daily totals.

Apple-Orange Waldorf Salad

Servings: 4

In 1893 the New York Waldorf Hotel introduced this salad to Americans.

2 tbs. reduced calorie mayonnaise
2 tbs. nonfat yogurt
2 tsp. honey
2 medium apples, diced
2 stalks celery, chopped
2 tbs. chopped walnuts
1 small orange, peeled, diced or 1/2 cup canned mandarin oranges

In a salad bowl, blend mayonnaise, yogurt and honey. Add apples, celery, walnuts and oranges; toss with dressing. Cover and chill in the refrigerator before serving.

Nutritional information per serving 158 calories, 28% calories from fat, 5 grams fat (1 1/4 tsp. fat), .8 grams saturated fat, 3 mg cholesterol, 2 grams protein, 30 grams carbohydrate, 65 mg sodium

Greek Pasta Salad

Servings: 2

Blue cheese or Roquefort could be substituted for the feta and then we would call this a French salad. In any case, just a small amount is necessary.

1/4 cup nonfat yogurt
1 clove garlic, minced
2 tsp. crumbled feta cheese
1 tsp. Dijon-style mustard
1/2 tsp. olive oil
4 black olives, chopped
1/2 green or red bell pepper, chopped
1 cup cauliflower, chopped
1 cup cooked pasta
freshly ground pepper to taste

In a salad bowl, mix together yogurt, garlic, cheese, mustard and olive oil. Add olives, green pepper, cauliflower and pasta; toss vegetables and pasta with dressing. Season with pepper and chill.

Nutritional information per serving 138 calories, 21% calories from fat, 3 grams fat (3/4 tsp. fat), .6 grams saturated fat, 2 mg cholesterol, 6 grams protein, 23 grams carbohydrate, 266 mg sodium

Overnight Layered Salad

Servings: 8

Be sure to dig down deep when you serve this classic salad, so everyone gets a portion of each layer.

1 medium head lettuce
1 (5 ozs.) can water chestnuts, sliced
4 green onions, sliced
4 stalks celery, sliced
3-4 medium tomatoes, chopped
1 (10 ozs.) pkg. frozen peas
½ cup reduced calorie mayonnaise
½ cup nonfat yogurt
1 tsp. dry mustard
¼ tsp. paprika
2 tbs. dry roasted sunflower seeds or chopped dry roasted peanuts

Use a clear glass bowl with straight sides. Wash lettuce and tear into bite-sized pieces. Spread over bottom of bowl. Scatter water chestnuts, green onions and celery over lettuce. Lay chopped tomatoes on top and spread peas over tomatoes. In a small bowl, combine mayonnaise, yogurt, mustard and paprika; spread over peas. Cover with plastic wrap and refrigerate for 4 hours or as long as 24 hours. Just before serving, remove plastic and scatter seeds on top.

Nutritional information per serving 134 calories, 40% calories from fat, 6 grams fat (1½ tsp. fat), 1 gram saturated fat, 5 mg cholesterol, 5 grams protein, 17 grams carbohydrate, 171 mg sodium

Oriental Zucchini Salad

Servings: 4

For a variety of shapes on the dinner table, cut zucchini into long, skinny match sticks instead of the usual rounds.

4 medium zucchini, sliced
2 green onions, chopped
1 small green bell pepper, diced
1 stalk celery, sliced
1/3 cup sugar
1/3 cup rice vinegar
2 tsp. sesame oil
1 tbs. reduced-sodium soy sauce

In a medium bowl, combine zucchini, onions, pepper and celery. In a small bowl, mix sugar, vinegar, oil and soy sauce; add to vegetables and stir. Chill for at least 1 hour, or prepare a day ahead and store in the refrigerator, stirring occasionally.

Nutritional information per serving 118 calories, 18% calories from fat, 3 grams fat (3/4 tsp. fat), 0 grams saturated fat, 0 mg cholesterol, 2 grams protein, 24 grams carbohydrate, 141 mg sodium

Spinach Salad Vinaigrette

Servings: 4

Three fruits—raspberry, orange and pear—combine to complement fresh spinach. Think about variations: substitute apple for pear and grapefruit for orange, and experiment with other flavored vinegars.

1 large bunch spinach
1 orange, peeled, sectioned
2 green onions, sliced
1 pear, thinly sliced
2 tbs. raspberry vinegar
2 tbs. orange juice
1 tsp. Dijon-style mustard
1 tsp. honey
2 tbs. olive oil

Wash, stem, cut and dry spinach. In a large bowl, combine spinach with orange, onions and pear; chill. In a small bowl, mix vinegar, orange juice, mustard, honey and oil. Just before serving, pour dressing over spinach and toss to coat well.

Nutritional information per serving 124 calories, 48% calories from fat, 7 grams fat (1 3/4 tsp. fat), 1 gram saturated fat, 0 mg cholesterol, 3 grams protein, 15 grams carbohydrate, 73 mg sodium

Rainbow Broccoli Salad

Servings: 4

Use this creamy salad dressing in any recipe that calls for a mayonnaise-type salad dressing.

2 cups chopped broccoli, steamed 1-2 minutes
1/4 red or yellow bell pepper, diced
2 green onions, thinly sliced
1/2 carrot, thinly sliced
1 medium tomato, chopped
1/4 cup nonfat yogurt
2 tbs. reduced calorie mayonnaise
1/2 tsp. dry mustard
1/2 tsp. dried dill weed
dash Tabasco sauce (optional)

In a salad bowl, combine broccoli, pepper, onion, carrot and tomato. In a small bowl, mix together yogurt, mayonnaise, mustard and dill. Pour over vegetables and toss. Cover and chill.

Nutritional information per serving 59 calories, 38% calories from fat, 3 grams fat (3/4 tsp. fat), .6 grams saturated fat, 3 mg cholesterol, 3 grams protein, 8 grams carbohydrate, 75 mg sodium

Mediterranean Bread Salad

Servings: 6

Fresh basil is a must for this refreshing summer salad.

3 cups ½" cubes stale French bread, toasted lightly
2 tomatoes, chopped
1-2 cucumbers or zucchini, chopped
½ cup finely chopped green onions
1 cup firmly packed fresh basil leaves
1 small garlic clove, minced or mashed
½ tsp. dry mustard
4 tbs. red wine vinegar
2 tbs. olive oil
1 tbs. Dijon-style mustard
freshly ground pepper to taste

In a large salad bowl, combine bread, tomatoes, cucumber and onion. In a blender or food processor, puree basil, garlic, mustard, vinegar and oil. Pour over bread and vegetables. Toss and season with pepper.

Nutritional information per serving 196 calories, 30% calories from fat, 7 grams fat (1¾ tsp. fat), 1 gram saturated fat, 0 mg cholesterol, 5 grams protein, 29 grams carbohydrate, 310 mg sodium

Zippy Garbanzo Salad

Servings: 4

If you don't like hot peppers, use red bell peppers. Mushrooms can also be added.

2 cups cooked or canned garbanzo beans
2 green onions, thinly sliced
1 small fresh jalapeño pepper, minced, or 2 tbs. diced canned green chiles
2 tbs. chopped fresh parsley
1 tbs. red wine vinegar
½ tsp. dry mustard
1 tbs. olive oil
1 tbs. grated Parmesan cheese
freshly ground pepper to taste

Rinse and drain beans, if using canned beans. In a salad bowl, combine beans, onions, minced pepper and parsley. In a small bowl, whisk together vinegar, mustard, oil and cheese; toss with beans. Season with ground pepper.

Nutritional information per serving 173 calories, 30% calories from fat, 6 grams fat (1½ tsp. fat), .9 grams saturated fat, 1 mg cholesterol, 8 grams protein, 23 grams carbohydrate, 61 mg sodium

Hot or Cold Seafood Salad

Servings: 4

Serve this versatile dish hot off the range in winter or make it ahead for a cool summer supper.

1 cup fresh or frozen peas
1 cup fresh or frozen pea pods
2 cups cooked converted rice
1 tomato, cubed
1 cup sliced mushrooms
1 (6 ozs.) can water-packed tuna, drained, or 6 ozs. cooked shrimp
2 green onions, sliced

In a large bowl, combine all ingredients. Pour dressing over all and toss gently to blend. Heat through or chill, depending on the season.

Dressing

2 tsp. low-sodium soy sauce
1 tsp. orange juice concentrate
1 tbs. sesame oil
2 tbs. rice vinegar
1 clove garlic, mashed
½ tsp. Dijon-style mustard

In a small bowl, combine all ingredients.

Nutritional information per serving 199 calories, 19% calories from fat, 4 grams fat (1 tsp. fat), 1 gram saturated fat, 24 mg cholesterol, 18 grams protein, 23 grams carbohydrate, 293 mg sodium

Dressing for Fruit Salads

Servings: 4

In 1934, Dorothy Neighbors, food editor of ***The Seattle Times****, put out a recipe bulletin that included this simple dressing. We took out the fat, and offer it for those times when you are tempted to put sweetened whipped cream over fruit or fruit gelatin.*

1 small ripe banana
2 tbs. powdered sugar
1 tsp. lemon juice
2 tbs. reduced calorie mayonnaise
1/2 cup nonfat yogurt

In a food processor or blender, combine ingredients and process until smooth.

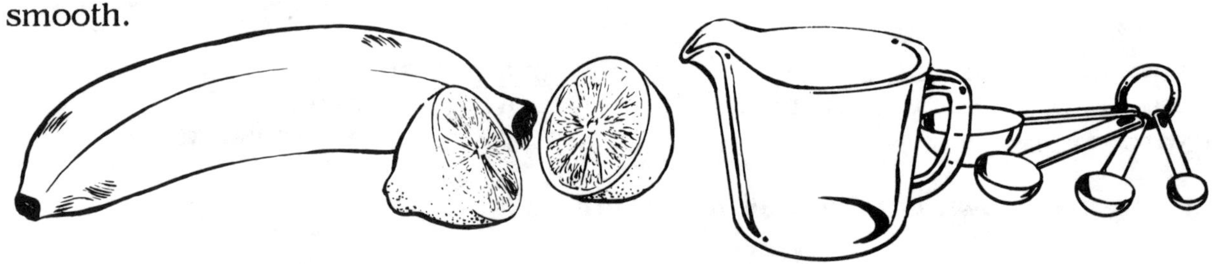

Nutritional information per serving 97 calories, 24% calories from fat, 3 grams fat (3/4 tsp. fat), 1 gram saturated fat, 3 mg cholesterol, 2 grams protein, 18 grams carbohydrate, 67 mg sodium

Dilled Potato Salad

Servings: 6

Don't waste time defrosting frozen peas. They can be added to the salad right from the freezer.

1/4 cup reduced calorie mayonnaise
1/4 cup nonfat yogurt
1 clove garlic, mashed or 1/4 tsp. garlic powder
2 tbs. chopped fresh dill weed or 1 tsp. dried
1/2 tsp. *each* salt-free seasoning blend and dried mustard
1 lb. (3 medium) red potatoes, cooked, cubed
1 cup frozen peas
2 green onions, chopped

In a large salad bowl, combine mayonnaise, yogurt and seasonings. Fold in potatoes, peas and onions. Cover and chill.

Nutritional information per serving 135 calories, 23% calories from fat, 4 grams fat (1 tsp. fat), .7 grams saturated fat, 4 mg cholesterol, 4 grams protein, 23 grams carbohydrate, 101 mg sodium

Beans and Grains

Beans and grains are among the oldest foods we know, and yet they are the health foods of the '90s. That makes them time-tested good nutrition. Beans and grains are high in complex carbohydrates and fiber, and low in fats and sodium. They contain no cholesterol. The soluble fiber in beans is similar to the fiber in oat bran that may reduce levels of blood cholesterol.

If you've never cooked beans before, it's really quite easy. Soak the beans overnight in water to cover; next day, drain and discard the water, cover with twice as much fresh cold water as you have beans, bring to a boil and simmer until the beans are soft but not mushy. Depending on the variety of the beans, cooking time can take from 1 to 2 hours. People in a hurry can find beans canned with reduced sodium, and canned beans are said to produce less flatulence.

Barley, rice, corn and pasta are only a few of the grain foods that are available to us today. As you reduce the amount of meat that you eat, look for and experiment with other grain foods like bulgar, whole wheat pastas, wheat berries, quinoa, millet and amaranth. Cooked beans and grains can be stored in the freezer without harm. However, they spoil in the refrigerator after 3 or 4 days.

Almost Boston Baked Beans

Servings: 6

Navy beans, the basic ingredient of baked beans, are rich in soluble fiber, the same fiber found in oat bran.

1 tbs. safflower oil
1/4 lb. mushrooms, sliced
2-3 cloves garlic, minced or mashed
2 tsp. dry mustard
2 green onions, chopped
5 cups cooked navy beans
1/4 cup jalapeño jelly
3 tbs. blackstrap molasses

Preheat oven to 300°. In a flame-proof casserole, heat oil; add mushrooms, garlic, mustard and green onions. Stir-fry until mushrooms are lightly browned. Add remaining ingredients and mix well. Cover and bake for 2 to 3 hours, stirring occasionally.

Nutritional information per serving 299 calories, 9% calories from fat, 3 grams fat (3/4 tsp. fat), .4 grams saturated fat, 0 mg cholesterol, 14 grams protein, 57 grams carbohydrate, 15 mg sodium

Refried Beans

Servings: 4

Most refried beans contain lard (saturated fat). It is easy to make a nutritious version without sacrificing flavor.

2 tsp. safflower or olive oil
1 small onion, chopped
2 cloves garlic, minced or mashed
2 cups cooked or canned pinto or kidney beans, drained
1⁄2 cup tomato sauce
1 tbs. Dijon-style mustard
2-3 drops Tabasco sauce or to taste
1⁄8 tsp. dried crushed red peppers or to taste

Heat a nonstick skillet; add oil; Add onion and garlic; cook until onion is soft, about 8 minutes. Add remaining ingredients and simmer for 5 minutes. Remove mixture from pan and mash with a fork. May be stored, covered, in the refrigerator up to 5 days.

Nutritional information per serving 157 calories, 17% calories from fat, 3 grams fat (3⁄4 tsp. fat), .3 grams saturated fat, 0 mg cholesterol, 9 grams protein, 25 grams carbohydrate, 237 mg sodium

Spicy Beans and Rice

Servings: 6

Centuries before the arrival of Europeans, Native Americans were growing beans. An early American favorite!

2 tsp. olive oil
1 onion, chopped
1-2 cloves garlic, minced, or 1/2 tsp. garlic powder
1 small zucchini, chopped
1 small carrot, chopped
1 cup salsa
1 cup cooked beans
2 cups cooked converted or brown rice
1 tbs. chili powder
1/4 cup grated reduced fat cheese (less than 5 grams fat per oz.)

Heat a nonstick skillet; add oil. Add onion, garlic, zucchini and carrot; cook over low heat until vegetables are soft. Add salsa and cook 5 minutes. Stir in beans, rice and seasoning; cook 5 minutes. Stir in cheese and heat until cheese melts.

Nutritional information per serving 164 calories, 17% calories from fat, 3 grams fat (3/4 tsp. fat), .8 grams saturated fat, 4 mg cholesterol, 6 grams protein, 28 grams carbohydrate, 260 mg sodium

Three Bean Salad

Servings: 6

Rinse canned beans under cold water and drain them to reduce sodium.

3 tbs. red wine vinegar
1-2 cloves garlic, minced or mashed
½ tsp. *each* dry mustard, chili powder, oregano
1-2 drops Tabasco sauce
2 tbs. olive oil
1 cup fresh or frozen corn
¼ cup chopped green onions
2 tbs. chopped fresh parsley
1 cup chopped celery
¼ cup canned diced green chiles
1 cup cooked or canned pinto or red beans, drained
1 cup cooked or canned garbanzo beans, drained
1 cup cooked or canned green or wax beans, drained

In a salad bowl, whisk together vinegar, seasonings and oil. Add vegetables, green chiles and beans; toss with dressing. Cover and marinate in refrigerator several hours.

Nutritional information per serving 231 calories, 27% calories from fat, 7 grams fat (1¾ tsp. fat), 1 gram saturated fat, 0 mg cholesterol, 10 grams protein, 35 grams carbohydrate, 123 mg sodium

Lentils with Almonds and Raisins

Servings: 4

We love lentils and were flattered when the Idaho-Washington Dry Pea and Lentil Commission featured our recipe at a cook-off in Sun Valley, Idaho.

1 tbs. olive oil
1 cup lentils, rinsed and drained
1 tsp. cinnamon
2½ cups defatted chicken stock
1 bay leaf
2 tbs. slivered almonds
¼ cup raisins or currants
½ cup nonfat yogurt
1 tsp. curry powder
⅛ tsp. cayenne pepper
freshly ground pepper to taste

Heat a nonstick skillet; add oil. Add lentils and cinnamon; stir-fry 2 to 3 minutes. Add stock and bay leaf; cover and cook over low heat for 30 minutes. Add almonds and raisins; continue cooking about 10 minutes or until lentils are soft. Combine yogurt, curry, cayenne and pepper; add to lentils and serve.

Nutritional information per serving 275 calories, 20% calories from fat, 6 grams fat (1½ tsp. fat), .7 grams saturated fat, .5 mg cholesterol, 19 grams protein, 39 grams carbohydrate, 176 mg sodium

Black Bean Soup

Servings: 8

If you like a thick soup, cook uncovered the last 30 minutes. Add more water or stock if you prefer a thinner soup.

1 tbs. olive oil
2 medium onions, chopped
2 carrots, chopped
1 cup chopped celery, including leaves
½ medium green pepper, chopped
4 cloves garlic, minced or mashed
3 cups black beans, soaked overnight
1 bay leaf
4-5 sprigs parsley, chopped
1 tsp. *each* oregano and dried thyme
zest of 1 orange
7-8 cups water
juice of 1 orange (optional)
2 tbs. dry sherry
1 tbs. Dijon-style mustard
freshly ground pepper to taste

In a large soup pot, heat olive oil. Add onions, carrots, celery, green pepper and garlic; cook over low heat until vegetables are soft. Drain beans and add to pot; add bay leaf, parsley, oregano, thyme, orange zest and water. Bring to a boil, reduce heat, cover and simmer about 2 hours. Uncover soup; add orange juice (if desired), mustard and sherry. Simmer uncovered for 20 to 30 minutes; remove bay leaf and add pepper before serving.

Nutritional information per 1-cup serving 241 calories, 10% calories from fat, 3 grams fat (¾ tsp. fat), .4 grams saturated fat, 0 mg cholesterol, 14 grams protein, 42 grams carbohydrate, 46 mg sodium

Lentil Soup

Servings: 8

Before cooking lentils, rinse well with cold water and pick out any tiny rocks that were inadvertently mixed in.

1 cup dried lentils
1 tbs. safflower oil
1 large onion, chopped
2 carrots, chopped
3/4 cup chopped celery, including leaves
1 turnip, chopped (optional)
2-3 cloves garlic, minced
1/2 tsp. *each* basil, oregano and paprika
1/2 cup converted rice
1/2 cup red wine
6-7 cups defatted chicken or vegetable stock
4 tbs. tomato paste
freshly ground pepper to taste

Rinse lentils and set aside. In a soup pot, heat oil; add onion, carrot, celery, turnip and garlic. Cook until soft, about 10 minutes. Add seasonings, rice and wine. Increase heat and stir for 3-4 minutes. Add stock, tomato paste and reserved lentils; bring soup to a boil, reduce heat, cover and simmer 1 hour. Season to taste with freshly ground pepper.

Nutritional information per 1-cup serving 189 calories, 11% calories from fat, 2 grams fat (1/2 tsp. fat), .2 grams saturated fat, 0 mg cholesterol, 12 grams protein, 29 grams carbohydrate, 211 mg sodium

Barley and Mushrooms

Servings: 4

You will always have defatted chicken stock ready to use if you keep a can of stock or broth in the refrigerator. When the can is opened, the fat will be easy to see because it will have risen to the top.

1 tbs. olive oil
2½ cups defatted chicken or vegetable stock
1 medium onion, finely chopped
2 cloves garlic, minced or mashed
½ lb. mushrooms, sliced
1 cup barley
½ cup canned green chiles, chopped
¼ tsp. dried crushed red chile peppers

Heat a nonstick skillet; add oil and 1 tbs. stock. Add onion, garlic and mushrooms; cook until golden. Add barley and stir-fry until barley begins to brown. Add remaining stock and chiles. Cover and cook over low heat for about 1 hour.

Nutritional information per serving 229 calories, 19% calories from fat, 5 grams fat (1¼ tsp. fat), .9 grams saturated fat, 0 mg cholesterol, 9 grams protein, 41 grams carbohydrate, 567 mg sodium

Pizza

Servings: 4

A vegetarian pizza cuts down on saturated fat and cholesterol, but not on flavor. We like whole wheat flour for its texture as well as its fiber, but this dough can be made with all white flour.

Pizza dough

½ cup warm water
1 tsp. dry yeast
⅛ tsp. sugar
¼ tsp. salt
1 tsp. olive oil
2 tbs. whole wheat flour
1-1½ cups all-purpose flour

Pour warm water into a mixing bowl. Add yeast and sugar; stir to dissolve yeast. Mix in salt and olive oil. Gradually add flour, stirring to make a soft workable dough. Add only enough flour to keep dough from sticking. Turn out onto a floured surface and knead until smooth and elastic, 7 to 10 minutes. Place dough in a greased bowl; cover with plastic wrap and towel. Let rise in a warm place until doubled, about 45 minutes. Punch dough down and roll out to fit a 12" pizza pan.

Topping

2 tsp. olive oil
1 tsp. garlic puree or 2 cloves garlic, mashed
3-4 green onions, chopped
1-1½ cups ***Quick Spaghetti Sauce,*** page 54
1 red or green bell pepper, chopped
¼ cup sliced mushrooms
4 ozs. reduced fat mozzarella cheese, grated
dried crushed red chile peppers (optional)

Preheat oven to 425°. Brush dough with olive oil and garlic puree. Scatter onions and press into dough. Pour on sauce; add vegetables and top with cheese. Bake for 20 minutes or until crust is brown and filling begins to bubble.

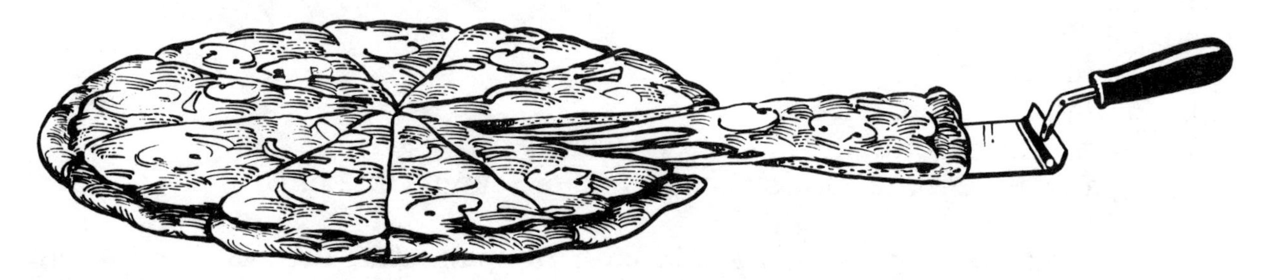

Nutritional information per serving 350 calories, 26% calories from fat, 10 grams fat (2¼ tsp. fat), 4 grams saturated fat, 15 mg cholesterol, 15 grams protein, 49 grams carbohydrate, 301 mg sodium

Meatless Lasagne

Servings: 8

The vegetables and sauce provide so much moisture that you don't need to cook the noodles before layering this casserole. Look for a prepared spaghetti sauce that contains no more than 2 grams of fat per 4-ounce serving. We tried and liked both Ragu Chunky Garden Style and Enrico brands.

1 (2 lbs.) jar meatless spaghetti sauce (or ***Quick Spaghetti Sauce***, page 54)
1 lb. lasagne noodles, made without eggs
3 cups diced zucchini or chopped fresh spinach
1 lb. lowfat ricotta cheese
1 egg white
1 tsp. salt-free Italian seasoning blend
1/2 tsp. garlic powder
1 tbs. grated Parmesan cheese
1 cup sliced mushrooms
1/4 cup grated reduced fat Swiss cheese (under 5 grams fat per oz.)

Preheat oven to 375°. Spread a thin layer of spaghetti sauce on the bottom of a 13"x9" baking dish. Cover with a layer of noodles. Scatter 1 cup of zucchini pieces over noodles; drizzle with spaghetti sauce. Cover with more noodles, zucchini and sauce. Beat ricotta cheese with egg white, seasoning blend, garlic powder and Parmesan cheese; carefully spread over casserole. Scatter mushrooms over cheese. Cover with 1 more layer of noodles, zucchini and sauce. (Save enough sauce so top can be completely covered.) Cover tightly with aluminum foil. Bake for 45 minutes to 1 hour. Uncover, scatter Swiss cheese on top and bake for 3 minutes more, just to melt cheese.

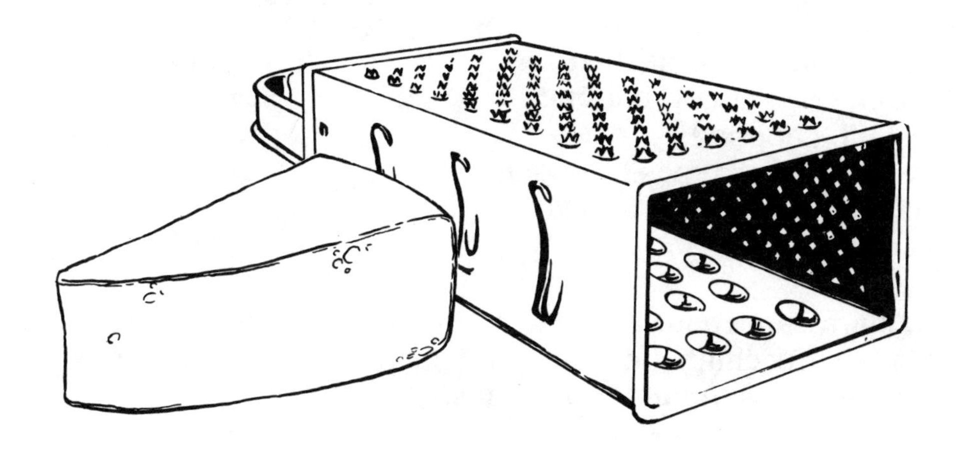

Nutritional information per serving 308 calories, 13% calories from fat, 5 grams fat (1¼ tsp. fat), 2 grams saturated fat, 23 mg cholesterol, 16 grams protein, 50 grams carbohydrate, 304 mg sodium

Quick Spaghetti Sauce

Servings: 6

This low-sodium spaghetti sauce may be used in any recipe from pizza to pasta, from fish to chicken.

2 tsp. olive oil
1 medium onion, chopped
2 cloves garlic, minced or mashed
1/2 small green bell pepper, chopped
1 small zucchini, chopped
1/2 tsp. *each* dry mustard, basil, oregano
2 cups tomato sauce, no salt added
1/4 cup red wine

Heat a medium saucepan; add oil. Add onion and garlic; cook until onion is soft. Add pepper, zucchini and seasonings; simmer 2 to 3 minutes. Add tomato sauce and red wine; simmer 20 minutes.

Nutritional information per 1/2-cup serving 52 calories, 27% calories from fat, 2 grams fat (1/2 tsp. fat), .2 grams saturated fat, 0 mg cholesterol, 2 grams protein, 9 grams carbohydrate, 18 mg sodium

Macaroni and Cheese

Servings: 6

Check cheese labels carefully. Reduced fat cheese should have no more than 5 grams of fat per ounce.

4 ozs. reduced fat cheddar cheese, grated (1 cup)
½ cup lowfat ricotta cheese or 1% fat cottage cheese
2 tbs. onion, minced
½ tsp. garlic powder
½ tsp. paprika
2 tbs. Dijon-style mustard
1 cup nonfat milk
2 tbs. oat bran or whole wheat bread crumbs
5 cups cooked pasta shells

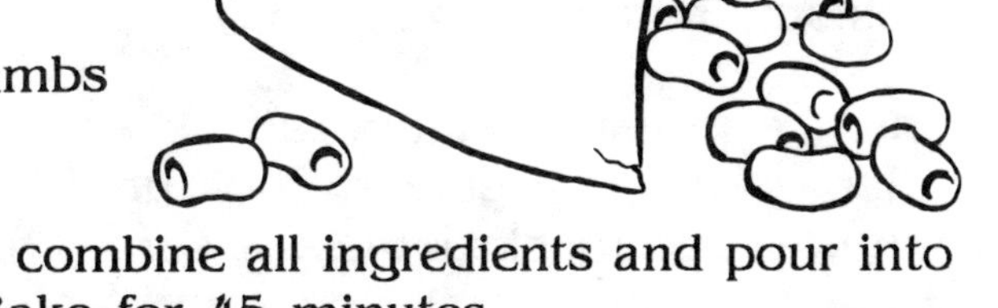

Preheat oven to 350°. In a large bowl, combine all ingredients and pour into a lightly greased 1½-quart casserole. Bake for 45 minutes.

Nutritional information per serving 327 calories, 19% calories from fat, 7 grams fat (1¾ tsp. fat), 4 grams saturated fat, 26 mg cholesterol, 19 grams protein, 48 grams carbohydrate, 349 mg sodium

Spinach Rice Pilaf

Servings: 4

This side dish could become a one-dish meal by adding a cup of cooked poultry, beans or leftover fish.

1 tbs. sesame seeds
2 tsp. safflower oil
1 medium onion, chopped
2 cloves garlic, minced or mashed
1 tsp. grated fresh ginger
1 bunch fresh spinach, washed, chopped or 1 (10 ozs.) pkg. frozen spinach, partially thawed
1/4 lb. mushrooms, sliced
1 cup converted rice
1-2 tbs. low sodium soy sauce
2 cups defatted chicken or vegetable stock
1/2 cup chopped water chestnuts (optional)

Heat a nonstick skillet; add sesame seeds and stir until toasted. Add oil, onion, garlic and ginger; cook until onion is soft. Add spinach and stir-fry 2 minutes; add mushrooms and stir-fry 3 to 4 minutes. Mix in rice, soy sauce and stock. Bring to a boil, cover and let simmer for 18 minutes. Remove lid and fluff with a fork. Garnish with chopped water chestnuts, if desired.

Nutritional information per serving 242 calories, 11% calories from fat, 3 grams fat (3/4 tsp. fat), .3 grams saturated fat, 0 mg cholesterol, 9 grams protein, 45 grams carbohydrate, 329 mg sodium

Indonesian Fried Rice

Servings: 2

Fried rice has become an American favorite. Our version borrows from Indonesian cuisine instead of the usual Chinese. Add leftover vegetables such as peas, broccoli or spinach to this dish, or substitute cooked fish or shrimp for the chicken.

½ tsp. sesame oil
2 green onions, chopped
⅓ cup chopped red bell pepper
1 clove garlic, minced
½ cup chopped mushrooms
½ cup diced cooked chicken or 1 (5 ozs.) can chicken
1 cup cooked converted rice
½ tsp. chili powder
¼ tsp. *each* ground coriander and ground cumin (or substitute ½ tsp. curry powder)
1 tbs. chopped dry roasted peanuts

Heat a nonstick skillet; add oil. Add onions, pepper, garlic and mushrooms. Cook until onions are translucent, about 4 minutes. Add chicken, rice, and seasonings; cook 5 minutes more, stirring constantly, until heated through. Serve at once with peanuts scattered on top.

Nutritional information per serving 193 calories, 20% calories from fat, 4 grams fat (1 tsp. fat), 1 gram saturated fat, 24 mg cholesterol, 14 grams protein, 25 grams carbohydrate, 41 mg sodium

Buttermilk Cornbread

Servings: 9

Buttermilk gives this cornbread a rich "down home" flavor.

2 cups yellow cornmeal
½ cup flour
2 tsp. baking powder
½ tsp. baking soda
1 tsp. minced dried onion (optional)
2 egg whites, beaten
2 cups nonfat buttermilk
1 tbs. safflower oil

Preheat oven to 400°. In a mixing bowl, combine dry ingredients. In another bowl, mix together beaten eggs, buttermilk and oil. Add wet ingredients to dry ingredients and mix just enough to moisten. Pour batter into a lightly greased nonstick 9" square baking pan. Bake for 20 to 25 minutes.

Nutritional information per serving 173 calories, 11% calories from fat, 2 grams fat (½ tsp. fat), 0 grams saturated fat, 1 mg cholesterol, 6 grams protein, 32 grams carbohydrate, 177 mg sodium

Meat

It's very American to describe a person as a "meat and potatoes" man or woman, but with the new guidelines for healthier eating, we should begin to say "potatoes with meat." Eating huge portions of meat with scanty vegetables alongside is out. Experts now tell us we should eat smaller portions of lean meat with larger portions of grains and vegetables.

Meat producers have responded by developing new strains of lean beef and pork. The U.S. Department of Agriculture, which controls the labeling on all meat that is shipped across state lines, has set standards for reduced fat meats. If a cut of meat is 25% lower in fat than the usual standard for that cut, it may be labeled "leaner" or "light;" the label must also include a statement of comparison with the standard. "Lean" or "lowfat" meat cannot contain more than 10% fat by weight; "extra lean" may not have more than 5%.

Because ground beef is generally ground at the retail store, USDA labels don't apply. Instead, ground beef standards are set by the states, and the standards vary greatly from state to state. Some states accept the USDA standards. Other states have no fat limits or labels, but instead use the terms "ground sirloin," "ground round," "ground top round" or "ground chuck." And some states use percentages of fat: "lean" ground beef may not exceed 23% fat, "extra lean" may not exceed 16%, and "leanest" may not exceed 9% fat. Talk to your butcher to find out what standards prevail in your meat market. If you can't find good ground meat, buy a roast or steak and have the butcher grind it for you, or grind it yourself at home.

Whether your meat is ground or whole, portion size should be no more than 4 ounces of cooked meat per person. All meat shrinks somewhat in cooking; for 4 ounces of cooked meat, you should start with 5 or 6 ounces of raw meat.

Swiss Steak

Servings: 6

Some of the new varieties of seasoned canned tomatoes—Cajun, Italian or Mexican—will add extra pizzazz to this old favorite.

1½ lbs. beef round steak, 1" thick
1 tsp. olive oil
⅓ cup flour
1 tsp. salt-free seasoning blend
freshly ground pepper to taste
1 large onion, sliced
½ green pepper, diced
1 (15 ozs.) can tomatoes

Trim all visible fat from meat. In a nonstick skillet, heat oil and brown meat on both sides. Remove meat from pan, pour off all fat and wipe pan with a paper towel. In a small bowl, combine flour, seasoning blend and pepper. Carefully brown this mix in the skillet over medium heat, stirring constantly to prevent burning. Return meat to pan and turn to coat both sides with browned flour. Add onion, green pepper and canned tomatoes. Bring to a boil, cover, reduce heat and cook for 1 hour or until tender. Remove meat and vegetables to a warm platter. Pour pan juices into a fat separator; serve defatted juices with meat.

Nutritional information per serving 277 calories, 34% calories from fat, 10 grams fat (2½ tsp. fat), 3 grams saturated fat, 93 mg cholesterol, 34 grams protein, 11 grams carbohydrate, 188 mg sodium

Pot Roast

Servings: 10

Oven roasting bags eliminate the need for browning meat in hot fat, and they collect all the wonderful cooking juices without burning them.

1 Reynolds brand oven cooking bag
1 tbs. flour
small oven rack
3 lbs. boneless beef rump or top round roast
2 bay leaves
1" cinnamon stick
6 cloves
1 onion, peeled, quartered
1 cup dry red wine (or substitute apple cider)
1 tbs. Worcestershire sauce

Preheat oven to 325°. Read manufacturer's instructions for the cooking bag. Shake flour in bag to coat inner surface and prevent bursting. Place bag in a deep roasting pan and lay the rack *inside* the bag. With a sharp knife, remove all visible fat from roast and carefully place roast on rack in bag. Scatter spices and onion around roast; pour wine and Worcestershire sauce into bottom of bag. Close bag with tie provided. Pierce top of bag in 6 places to allow steam to escape. Bake for 2 hours. Take pan from oven, carefully slit bag and remove roast to a warm platter. Cover with foil to keep warm. Pour pan juices into a fat separator and set aside until fat has risen to the top. Serve defatted pan juices with meat; discard fat.

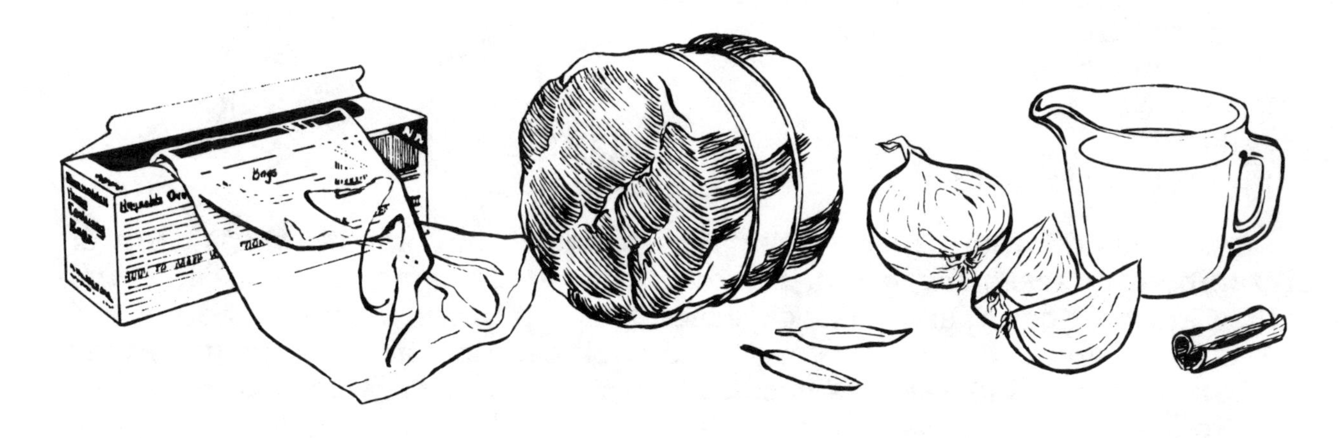

Nutritional information per serving 270 calories, 32% calories from fat, 9 grams fat (2¼ tsp. fat), 3 grams saturated fat, 94 mg cholesterol, 41 grams protein, 2 grams carbohydrate, 85 mg sodium

Chicken-Fried Steak

Servings: 2

Choose the leanest beef you can find, because the cooking method seals in the naturally occurring fat in the meat.

2 (6 ozs. each) lean beef cube steaks (or use veal or turkey)
1⁄3 cup wheat germ or fine cracker crumbs
1 tsp. salt-free seasoning blend
1 egg white beaten with 1 tbs. water
1 tsp. olive oil
water
1 medium onion, sliced

Pat steaks dry with paper towels. In a shallow dish, combine wheat germ or crumbs with seasoning blend. Dip each cube steak in beaten egg white and then in wheat germ. In a nonstick skillet, heat oil. Brown steaks on both sides. Add onion and 1 tbs. water, cover, and cook over low heat 20 minutes, until meat is tender. Add water as necessary. Serve each steak with onions heaped on top.

Nutritional information per serving 349 calories, 35% calories from fat, 14 grams fat (3½ tsp. fat), 4 grams saturated fat, 94 mg cholesterol, 40 grams protein, 16 grams carbohydrate, 111 mg sodium

Beef Stroganoff

Servings: 4

For an even leaner dish, substitute turkey breast for beef.

1 lb. lean beef, flank or round steak, cut into 1" cubes
1/4 tsp. olive oil
1 small onion, chopped
1 cup sliced mushrooms
1 tbs. flour
1/2 cup defatted chicken stock
1/2 tsp. *each* garlic powder, dry mustard, paprika
1 tsp. Worcestershire sauce
1 cup nonfat yogurt
4 cups cooked noodles (made without eggs)

Heat a nonstick skillet; quickly brown beef cubes. Drain beef on several thicknesses of paper towels, and wipe skillet clean of fat. Spread oil over skillet and cook onion and mushrooms until soft. Sprinkle flour over vegetables and mix it in. Transfer vegetables to a small bowl and set aside. Return beef to skillet, add stock and seasonings, and bring to a boil. Cover and simmer 20 to 25 minutes, until meat is tender. Add cooked vegetables to meat for the last 5 or 10 minutes. Just before serving, stir in yogurt; do not boil. Serve over noodles.

Nutritional information per serving 467 calories, 20% calories from fat, 10 grams fat (2 1/2 tsp. fat), 4 grams saturated fat, 94 mg cholesterol, 44 grams protein, 48 grams carbohydrate, 191 mg sodium

Hamburgers

Servings: 4

Even in this leannest of hamburger patties, there is still a high percentage of fat. That's why the sandwich you make can include mustard, sprouts, lettuce, tomato or pickle, but no fatty additions like cheese or mayonnaise.

½ lb. ground turkey
½ lb. extra lean ground beef
¼ cup fine bread crumbs or matzo meal
¼ cup grated or finely chopped onion
1 egg white beaten with 2 tbs. water
1 tsp. salt-free seasoning blend
½ tsp. garlic powder
½ tsp. dry mustard
¼ tsp. freshly ground pepper
4 whole wheat hamburger buns
4 lettuce leaves
4 slices tomato
2 tsp. relish

Preheat grill or broiler. In a large bowl, combine meats, bread crumbs, onion, egg white and seasonings. Form into 4 patties. Grill over charcoal or broil in the oven for approximately 3 minutes on each side, or to taste. Serve on hamburger buns, adding lettuce, tomato and ½ tsp. relish to each hamburger.

Nutritional information per serving 346 calories, 37% calories from fat, 14 grams fat (3½ tsp. fat), 5 grams saturated fat, 61 mg cholesterol, 24 grams protein, 30 grams carbohydrate, 420 mg sodium

Meat Loaf

Servings: 4

There are a number of ways to bake meat loaf so that the fat drains off. Bake it on a broiler-pan rack with a drip pan beneath it; buy a special meat loaf pan with a double bottom to collect fat; or create your own double-bottomed meat loaf pan with aluminum foil.

½ lb. ground turkey
½ lb. extra lean ground beef
½ cup uncooked oatmeal
1 (6 ozs.) can V–8 vegetable juice
1 egg white
½ cup chopped onion
1 clove garlic, finely minced
1 tsp. *each* chili powder and dry mustard
2 tsp. salt-free seasoning blend
4 tbs. tomato paste, divided

Preheat oven to 350°. In a mixing bowl, combine meats, oatmeal, juice, egg white, onion, garlic, seasonings and 2 tbs. tomato paste until well mixed. Bake as suggested above, or in a nonstick loaf pan. Spread remaining tomato paste on top before baking. Bake 1 hour. Let stand 5 minutes before slicing.

Nutritional information per serving 249 calories, 44% calories from fat, 12 grams fat (3 tsp. fat), 4 grams saturated fat, 61 mg cholesterol, 22 grams protein, 14 grams carbohydrate, 247 mg sodium

Chili Con Carne for a Crowd

Servings: 12

This recipe was clipped from ***The Louisville Courier-Journal*** *in the '50s. We have adapted it to fit the nutritional standards of the '90s.*

1 lb. ground turkey
½ lb. extra lean ground beef
4 large onions, chopped
4 cloves garlic, minced or mashed
2 (28 ozs. each) cans tomatoes
1 (6 ozs.) can tomato paste
6 cups cooked or canned kidney beans, drained (1 cup liquid reserved)
1 cup beer
6 tbs. chili powder
¼ tsp. dried crushed chili peppers (optional)

Heat a large saucepan. Brown meat and drain on paper towels. Discard all but 1 tsp. liquid remaining in pan. Add onions and garlic; cook. Add remaining ingredients, meat and 1 cup bean liquid. Break up tomatoes with a fork. Simmer chili uncovered for 30 minutes. Cover and simmer 30 minutes more. Adjust seasonings, as chili powders will vary.

Nutritional information per serving 268 calories, 20% calories from fat, 6 grams fat (1½ tsp. fat), 2 grams saturated fat, 29 mg cholesterol, 20 grams protein, 36 grams carbohydrate, 305 mg sodium

Spaghetti with Meat Sauce

Servings: 4

In this meat sauce the ground beef has been reduced to 1⁄2 lb. and vegetables substituted for the missing beef. You could also use 1⁄4 lb. ground turkey and 1⁄4 lb. ground beef.

1⁄2 lb. lean ground beef
1 small onion, chopped
1 small zucchini, chopped
2 cloves garlic, minced or mashed
1⁄2 red or green bell pepper, chopped
1⁄4 lb. mushrooms, chopped
2 cups ***Spaghetti Sauce,*** page 54, or canned tomato sauce
1⁄4 cup canned diced green chilies (or to taste)
1 tsp. dried leaf basil or oregano
1⁄2 tsp. chili powder (optional)
2 cups cooked pasta

In a large nonstick skillet, brown meat. Drain meat on paper towels. Discard all but 1⁄2 tsp. of liquid remaining in pan. Add onion, zucchini, garlic and peppers; cook until onion is soft. Add mushrooms and stir-fry 3 to 5 minutes. Stir in meat, tomato sauce, green chilies and seasoning. Simmer for 15 minutes. Serve over pasta.

Nutritional information per serving 262 calories, 30% calories from fat, 9 grams fat (2 1⁄4 tsp. fat), 3 grams saturated fat, 37 mg cholesterol, 16 grams protein, 32 grams carbohydrate, 287 mg sodium

Chicken and Turkey

Most of the fat and cholesterol in chicken and turkey is in the skin. If you wait to discard the skin until after the poultry is cooked, you lose all the good flavors of the seasoning that you cooked with. Remove the skin *before* you cook.

Skinless chicken or turkey breast is almost as low in fat as fish. You can substitute these white meats in any of your recipes that call for veal cutlets or sliced beef round or flank steak. Ground turkey and chicken are now generally available in stores, but these products contain a combination of white and dark meats, making them higher in fat than white meat alone. For the leanest meat, buy turkey or chicken breasts, skin them and grind them yourself.

Chicken with Italian Sauce

Servings: 4

The tantalizing smell of simmering Italian tomato sauce adds to the pleasure.

1 tsp. olive oil
2 whole chicken breasts, skin removed
1 medium onion, finely chopped
2-3 cloves garlic, minced or mashed
1 cup sliced mushrooms
1/2 green or red bell pepper, finely chopped
1 tsp. dry mustard
1/2 tsp. *each* dried leaf basil and oregano
1 cup tomato sauce
2 cups cooked pasta or grains

Brush a nonstick skillet with oil; heat. Brown chicken and set aside. In the same pan, cook onion, garlic and mushrooms until onion is golden; add peppers and stir-fry 3 to 4 minutes. Add seasonings and sauce. Return chicken with its juices to pan. Cover pan and cook until chicken is tender, 20 to 30 minutes. Serve over pasta or grains.

Nutritional information per serving 258 calories, 11% calories from fat, 3 grams fat (3/4 tsp. fat), .6 grams saturated fat, 68 mg cholesterol, 31 grams protein, 25 grams carbohydrate, 449 mg sodium

Curried Chicken

Servings: 4

We like to serve the sauce over rice and surround it with the chicken and fruit.

1 tsp. polyunsaturated margarine
2 whole chicken breasts or 4 thighs, skin removed
2 tbs. curry powder
1 medium onion, chopped
2 cloves garlic, finely chopped
1 (5 ozs.) can sliced water chestnuts
1 medium tart green apple, diced
1 small banana, diced
½ cup canned chunk pineapple, no sugar added
1 tbs. tomato paste
1 cup defatted chicken stock
mint leaves for garnish (optional)

Heat a nonstick skillet; melt margarine. Add chicken and slowly brown. Sprinkle with curry powder. Remove chicken and set aside; add onion, garlic and water chestnuts to skillet. Stir and cook for 3 minutes. Add apple, banana, pineapple, tomato paste and chicken stock to skillet. Return chicken to skillet. Cover and cook for 20 minutes. Uncover and cook for 15 minutes. Serve garnished with mint, if desired.

Nutritional information per serving 275 calories, 11% calories from fat, 3 grams fat (¾ tsp. fat), .1 gram saturated fat, 70 mg cholesterol, 30 grams protein, 32 grams carbohydrate, 154 mg sodium

Oven-Fried Chicken

Servings: 4

Panko is Japanese-style bread crumbs. It can usually be found in the ethnic foods section of the supermarket. Look for a brand that is made without oil or shortening. Ordinary bread crumbs may be used, but again, check the label for fats.

2 egg whites
2 tbs. nonfat milk
1/4 cup all-purpose flour
1/4 tsp. *each* dry mustard, garlic powder and pepper
1/2 tsp. minced dried onions
1/2 tsp. paprika
whole chicken breasts, split, skin removed
2 cups panko or plain bread crumbs
1 tsp. salt-free seasoning blend
1 tsp. safflower oil

Preheat oven to 425°. In a shallow bowl, combine egg whites and milk; set aside. In a paper bag, combine flour, dry mustard, garlic powder, pepper, dried onions and paprika. In another paper bag, combine panko or bread crumbs and salt-free seasoning blend. Place chicken in bag with flour and shake to coat; remove and dip in egg mixture. Place chicken in second bag and shake to coat with crumbs. Brush oil on a nonstick baking pan; add chicken and bake 20 minutes. Turn and bake 20 to 30 minutes or until chicken is tender and crisp.

Nutritional information per serving 202 calories, 15% calories from fat, 3 grams fat (3/4 tsp. fat), .7 grams saturated fat, 49 mg cholesterol, 24 grams protein, 18 grams carbohydrate, 199 mg sodium

Quick Oven-Fried Chicken for Two

Servings: 2

Crispy chicken can still be part of your diet, even when you're cutting down on fat.

2 servings favorite chicken parts (4-5 ozs. each serving)
1/4 cup corn meal or fine bread crumbs
1/2 tsp. chili powder
1/4 tsp. *each* onion and garlic powder
freshly ground pepper to taste
1 egg white, beaten
1/2 tsp. corn oil

Preheat oven to 350°. Remove skin and visible fat from chicken parts. In a paper bag, combine cornmeal and seasonings. Dip chicken in egg white and then shake in bag to coat with cornmeal. Oil a shallow baking pan and arrange chicken parts in pan. Bake for 45 to 50 minutes or until chicken is done, turning once to brown both sides.

Nutritional information per serving 213 calories, 18% calories from fat, 4 grams fat (1 tsp. fat), 1 gram saturated fat, 77 mg cholesterol, 28 grams protein, 14 grams carbohydrate, 114 mg sodium

Honey-Citrus Chicken

Servings: 4

This is a very sweet way to prepare chicken. Continue the citrus theme with a spinach-orange salad or steamed Brussels sprouts tossed with mandarin oranges.

2 breasts of chicken, split
½ cup orange juice
1 cup fine bread crumbs
1 tbs. grated orange rind
½ tsp. salt-free seasoning blend
defatted chicken stock or water
2 tbs. lemon juice
½ cup honey

Preheat oven to 350°. Remove skin and all visible fat from chicken. In a shallow dish, pour orange juice. In another shallow dish, combine bread crumbs, orange rind and seasoning. Dip chicken in juice and then roll in crumbs. Arrange pieces in a shallow pan and bake for 30 minutes. Pour remaining orange juice into a measuring cup and add stock or water to make ¾ cup. Combine with lemon juice and honey in a small pan and heat until mixed. Pour orange-honey over chicken and bake for 30 minutes more, basting occasionally.

Nutritional information per serving 206 calories, 7% calories from fat, 2 grams fat (½ tsp. fat), 0 grams saturated fat, 49 mg cholesterol, 21 grams protein, 27 grams carbohydrate, 129 mg sodium

Dijonnaise Chicken

Servings: 4

The mustard coating gives chicken tangy flavor and golden color. Guests will never notice that the skin is missing.

2 whole chicken breasts, skin removed
2 tbs. *each* Dijon-style mustard and coarse ground prepared mustard
freshly ground pepper to taste
½ cup dry white wine
½ cup lowfat ricotta cheese
1 cup seedless red grapes

Preheat oven to 350°. In a shallow pan or flame-proof casserole that will hold chicken pieces in one layer, combine mustards. Place chicken in pan and coat with mustard. Sprinkle with pepper. Cover and marinate for 1 hour at room temperature or overnight in the refrigerator. Pour wine into pan; bake uncovered for 30 minutes or until chicken is tender and golden. Baste occasionally. Remove chicken and keep warm. Place casserole over burner and bring juices to a boil. Stir in cheese. Return chicken to pan, add grapes and heat 5 minutes. Spoon sauce over chicken.

Nutritional information per serving 210 calories, 14% calories from fat, 3 grams fat (¾ tsp. fat), .8 grams saturated fat, 73 mg cholesterol, 30 grams protein, 10 grams carbohydrate, 436 mg sodium

Grilled Chicken

Servings: 4

Use the same method for each of these recipes. In a small saucepan, combine all ingredients except chicken. Pour sauce over chicken and marinate 30 minutes at room temperature or overnight in the refrigerator. Prepare grill or turn on broiler. Place chicken on hot grill and brush with marinade. Grill until chicken is tender, 15 to 20 minutes. The recipes may be doubled to serve a crowd.

Jalapeño and Mustard Sauce

1/2 cup jalapeño jelly or apricot preserves
1/4 cup coarse ground mustard
2 tbs. lemon juice
2 whole chicken breasts, skin removed

Nutritional information per serving 156 calories, 10% calories from fat, 2 grams fat (1/2 tsp. fat), .3 grams saturated fat, 49 mg cholesterol, 20 grams protein, 14 grams carbohydrate, 254 mg sodium

Salsa and Mustard Sauce

1/2 cup salsa
2 tbs. coarse ground mustard
1/2 tsp. garlic powder
2 whole chicken breasts, skin removed

Nutritional information per serving 112 calories, 13% calories from fat, 2 grams fat (1/2 tsp. fat), .3 grams saturated fat, 49 mg cholesterol, 20 grams protein, 3 grams carbohydrate, 313 mg sodium

Vegetarian Dressings

These fat-free dressings roast alongside the turkey, not in it, so the vegetarian in the family can also share in the Thanksgiving Day feast without guilt.

Sweet Vegetarian Dressing

Servings: 10

- 1/4 cup dried vegetable flakes
- 4 cups boiling water
- 1 tsp. olive oil
- 1 cup *each* diced onion and diced celery
- 2 tart apples, diced
- 1 cup dried apricots, quartered
- 3 tbs. poultry seasoning, or substitute 1 tbs. *each* dried sage, rosemary and thyme
- 1 tsp. freshly ground pepper
- 1 cup raisins
- 8 cups diced toasted whole wheat bread

Preheat oven to 350°. In a medium bowl, stir vegetable flakes into boiling water and set aside for 15 minutes. Heat a nonstick skillet; add oil. Add onions and celery, cook until golden and transfer to a large bowl. Add apples, apricots, seasonings, raisins and bread cubes; mix well. Pour vegetable broth over bread and stir until thoroughly dampened. Spoon into a lightly greased casserole, cover tightly with foil and bake for 1 hour.

Nutritional information per serving 192 calories, 8% calories from fat, 2 grams fat (1/2 tsp. fat), 0 grams saturated fat, 0 mg cholesterol, 4 grams protein, 42 grams carbohydrate, 140 mg sodium

Savory Variation

Servings: 10

Omit apples, apricots and raisins. Add 1 cup coarsely chopped mushrooms, 1/2 cup chopped parsley and 1 (5 ozs.) can water chestnuts, drained and coarsely chopped.

Nutritional information per serving 90 calories, 15% calories from fat, 2 grams fat (1/2 tsp. fat), 0 grams saturated fat, 0 mg cholesterol, 3 grams protein, 17 grams carbohydrate, 137 mg sodium

Whole Wheat / Mushroom Dressing

Servings: 8

Check the label on whole wheat bread to make certain that whole wheat flour is listed as the first or second ingredient.

1 oz. dried mushrooms
1/4 cup dry sherry
2 tsp. safflower oil
1 medium onion, chopped
1 cup chopped celery, including leaves
1-2 cloves garlic, chopped
1 lb. fresh mushrooms, chopped
1/2 tsp. *each* sage, thyme, oregano and marjoram, or 2 tsp. poultry seasoning
8-10 cups cubed toasted whole wheat bread
1 1/2-2 cups defatted chicken or vegetable stock

Preheat oven to 350°. In a small bowl, soak dried mushrooms in sherry for 2 hours; drain, reserving sherry. Chop mushrooms. Heat a nonstick skillet; add oil. Add onion and celery and cook for 5 minutes. Add garlic and cook 1 minute. Add fresh mushrooms and seasoning and stir-fry for 5 minutes; add dried mushrooms and cook 1 minute. In a large bowl, combine cooked vegetables and toasted bread. Pour in stock and reserved sherry; mix. Pour into a lightly greased baking pan and bake covered for 45 minutes. Uncover and bake 15 minutes more.

Nutritional information per serving 137 calories, 18% calories from fat, 3 grams fat (3/4 tsp. fat), .6 grams saturated fat, 0 mg cholesterol, 5 grams protein, 22 grams carbohydrate, 216 mg sodium

Post-Thanksgiving Scramble

Servings: 4

This quickie will provide one of those Thanksgiving weekend meals when you're too busy or lazy to cook, whether you're occupied with shopping, raking leaves or watching a football game.

½ tsp. olive oil
½ cup chopped onion
¼ cup defatted turkey or chicken stock
2 cups diced roasted turkey
2 cups leftover turkey dressing, made without fat
2 tsp. sweet mustard

Heat a nonstick skillet; add olive oil. Add onion and cook until golden. As onion becomes dry, add stock a spoonful at a time. Add turkey to skillet, cooking and stirring to heat and brown. Keep adding stock so that mix does not burn. Add stuffing and stir in remaining stock. Just before serving, mix in mustard.

Nutritional information per serving 223 calories, 24% calories from fat, 6 grams fat (1½ tsp. fat), 2 grams saturated fat, 54 mg cholesterol, 24 grams protein, 19 grams carbohydrate, 221 mg sodium

Turkey or Chicken Mock Soufflé

Servings: 8

Old cookbooks sometimes refer to casseroles like this as "strata," or layers.

8 slices day-old bread, quartered
2 cups diced cooked turkey or chicken
½ cup chopped onion
½ cup chopped celery
½ cup chopped mushrooms
½ cup nonfat yogurt
1 tbs. Dijon-style mustard
imitation eggs equivalent to 2 eggs
1½ cup nonfat milk
2 tsp. salt-free seasoning blend
¼ cup reduced calorie mayonnaise

Arrange half the bread quarters to cover the bottom of a 9" square baking dish. In a large bowl, combine turkey, onion, celery, mushrooms and yogurt, and spread over bread. Arrange remaining bread quarters over turkey mix. In another bowl, stir mustard, imitation eggs, milk and seasoning blend together; pour over bread quarters, moistening all of them. Cover with plastic wrap and refrigerate overnight or for at least 6 hours. Next day, preheat oven to 325°. Remove plastic and spread mayonnaise over all. Bake for 1 hour.

Nutritional information per serving 214 calories, 22% calories from fat, 5 grams fat (1¼ tsp. fat), 1 gram saturated fat, 30 mg cholesterol, 18 grams protein, 23 grams carbohydrate, 341 mg sodium

Turkey Rice Soup

Servings: 8

If cooking turkey soup after a turkey dinner doesn't sound appealing, freeze the carcass and cook at a later day. Just remember to cook the soup one day before serving so that all fat can be removed.

1 turkey carcass
2 cups chopped celery, including leaves
4 carrots, chopped
2 medium onions, chopped
1 turnip, chopped
3-4 cloves garlic, coarsely chopped
6-8 sprigs parsley, including stems
6 peppercorns
1 tsp. dry mustard
1 tsp cider or red wine vinegar
1 cup converted rice
8-10 cups water

In a large soup pot, combine all ingredients except rice. Cover with water, bring to a boil, reduce heat, cover and simmer for 2 to 3 hours. Remove carcass and scrape meat from bones. Set meat aside; cool soup and place in refrigerator. Next day remove fat from soup; discard. Bring soup to a boil and add meat and rice. Simmer covered for 30 to 45 minutes. Serve hot.

Nutritional information per serving 183 calories, 10% calories from fat, 2 grams fat (1⁄2 tsp. fat), .6 grams saturated fat, 27 mg cholesterol, 13 grams protein, 28 grams carbohydrate, 65 mg sodium

Golden Autumn Soup

Servings: 4

Sweet potatoes give this soup its rich color. Substitute cooked squash, pumpkin or rutabaga for the same golden look.

2 cups defatted turkey stock or canned chicken stock
1 cup diced cooked sweet potato
1 onion, chopped
1 clove garlic, minced
1/4 cup chopped celery, including leaves
1-2 sprigs fresh parsley, including stems
1/4 tsp. dried thyme
1 bay leaf
freshly grated pepper to taste
1 cup diced cooked turkey

In a large soup pot, combine all ingredients except turkey. Cook until vegetables are tender. Remove bay leaf and parsley stems. Puree in a food processor or blender, if desired. Add turkey pieces and heat through.

Nutritional information per serving 220 calories, 15% calories from fat, 2 grams fat (1/2 tsp. fat), 1 gram saturated fat, 27 mg cholesterol, 13 grams protein, 10 grams carbohydrate, 148 mg sodium

Turkey Noodle Dinner

Servings: 4

Noodles come in such a great variety of shapes, sizes and colors these days. Why serve a tan or beige casserole, when you can have one in multi-colors?

1 onion, chopped
½ cup chopped green pepper
1 cup sliced mushrooms
¼ cup chopped parsley
¼ cup defatted turkey or chicken stock
1 tbs. flour
2 cups cubed cooked turkey or chicken
1 cup nonfat yogurt
½ tsp. dry mustard
½ tsp. salt-free seasoning blend
2 cups cooked noodles (without eggs)

In a large nonstick skillet, cook onions, pepper, mushrooms and parsley in a small amount of stock until vegetables are soft. Sprinkle flour over vegetables, add remaining stock and cook, stirring until thickened. Add turkey and heat through. Add yogurt, seasoning, mustard and noodles; mix well (do not boil).

Nutritional information per serving 251 calories, 10% calories from fat, 3 grams fat (¾ tsp. fat), 1 gram saturated fat, 50 mg cholesterol, 29 grams protein, 26 grams carbohydrate, 151 mg sodium

Fish

Fish and seafood are naturally low in saturated fat. If you are eating fish in order to reduce fat in your diet, you should not use cooking methods that add fats to a very healthy food. Do not fry or sauté fish in any kind of fat. Fish, to remain a lowfat food, should be baked, poached, steamed, grilled, stir-fried or microwaved.

Omega-3, a phrase we hear often in discussions of cholesterol-lowering diets, is a fatty acid found in fish oil. Certain populations who eat a diet high in omega-3 (like Greenland Eskimos and Japanese fishermen) have less coronary heart disease than other, similar groups who don't eat fish. However, the relationship between fish oil and heart attacks is not clear, and researchers warn us not to jump to conclusions. Instead, they urge us to eat small portions of fish, 3 to 4 ounces, two or more times a week.

In our recipes, we do not specify a certain kind of fish because there are so many different varieties available in different parts of the country. We prefer to give you methods of cooking fish steaks, fillets or whole fish that you can use with the freshest fish in your area.

Wherever you are, storing fish properly is most important to a successful finished dish. Fish should always be kept cold. Wait to buy fish as the last item in the supermarket. As soon as you get home, unwrap the fish, rinse it under cold running water, and lay it on ice in the refrigerator. Don't let the fish sit out at room temperature waiting to be cooked.

Stuffed Whole Fish

Servings: 2

To estimate the time a whole fish should bake, lay the fish on its side and measure the fattest part. Allow 13 minutes per inch: a 3" fish should bake for about 39 minutes. To test fish for doneness, draw a knife down the line along the side in the fattest part. Look at the open cut; the flesh should look opaque, not bloody or translucent.

½ tsp. olive oil
1 tbs. *each* finely chopped onion, celery, parsley and mushrooms
¾ cup fresh bread crumbs
¼ tsp. dried thyme
1 egg white, slightly beaten
2 (9 ozs. each) trout, or 1 whole fish (about 1½ lbs.)

Preheat oven to 350°. Heat a nonstick skillet; add oil. Add onion, celery, parsley and mushrooms; cook until soft. Stir in crumbs and thyme. Remove from heat and add egg white; mix well. Set aside. Rinse fish inside and out and pat dry. Lay fish on a square of aluminum foil large enough to enclose it completely. Stuff crumb mixture into fish. Wrap fish in foil, closing all ends tightly. Bake for about 20 minutes, or for a larger fish, about 30 minutes.

Nutritional information per serving 281 calories, 26% calories from fat, 8 grams fat (2 tsp. fat), 2 grams saturated fat, 103 mg cholesterol, 41 grams protein, 9 grams carbohydrate, 163 mg sodium

Steamed Fish with Peanut Sauce

Servings: 4

If you don't have a steamer, use an empty tuna can which has the top and bottom lid removed as a support for raising the dish above the level of boiling water.

4 fish fillets (4 ozs. each)
2-3 green onions, finely chopped
1 tsp. grated fresh ginger
2 tbs. sherry
2 tbs. orange juice concentrate or marmalade
peanut sauce

Arrange fish on a heat-proof plate. Sprinkle with onions, ginger, sherry and orange juice. Place dish on a steamer over boiling water. Cover and steam about 15 minutes or until fish flakes when tested with a folk, about 15 minutes. Pour peanut sauce over fish and serve.

Peanut Sauce

1 tbs. peanut butter, 100% peanuts, no salt added
1 tbs. orange juice concentrate
1 tbs. red wine or cider vinegar
1/4 tsp. fresh grated ginger
1/4 tsp. chili powder
1/4 tsp. garlic powder or puree
2 tsp. low-sodium soy sauce

In a small saucepan, combine all ingredients and simmer 2-3 minutes.

Nutritional information per serving 207 calories, 24% calories from fat, 5 grams fat (1 1/4 tsp. fat), .8 grams saturated fat, 47 mg cholesterol, 27 grams protein, 7 grams carbohydrate, 167 mg sodium

Microwaved Steamed Fish

Servings: 4

Foods in a microwave oven cook in a ring. Keep the center of the dish empty and thicker pieces on the outside edge for even cooking.

½ cup *each* sliced celery, onion, carrots
1 bay leaf
10 whole peppercorns
¼ cup water
1 lb. fish fillets (cod, flounder, perch, halibut)
¼ cup lemon juice
1 tsp. low-sodium soy sauce
¾ tsp. grated fresh ginger
1 clove garlic, minced
2 tsp. cornstarch dissolved in 2 tsp. water
1 tsp. sesame oil

Arrange celery, onion, carrots, bay leaf and peppercorns around the edge of a 9" round microwavable dish. Add water. Cover with plastic wrap, leaving a small vent to allow steam to escape, and microwave on high for 3 minutes. Arrange fish fillets over vegetables with thicker edges toward outside of dish.

Sprinkle fish with 2 tsp. lemon juice, cover with plastic wrap leaving a vent, and microwave on high for 4-7 minutes. Turn dish once. Fish is done when no part looks pink or translucent. Let fish stand covered for 5 minutes. Pour pan juices into a large microwavable measuring cup; add water to make 3/4 cup. Stir in remaining lemon juice, soy sauce, ginger, garlic and cornstarch. Microwave on high 3 minutes, until mixture boils and thickens. Stir in sesame oil. Arrange fish on a platter. Remove bay leaf and peppercorns and stir vegetables into sauce. Pour sauce over fish and serve.

Nutritional information per serving 185 calories, 23% calories from fat, 5 grams fat (1¼ tsp. fat), 1 gram saturated fat, 46 mg cholesterol, 26 grams protein, 6 grams carbohydrate, 139 mg sodium

Quick Broiled Fish

Servings: 4

You can vary the flavor of this dish by changing seasonings. For example use curry, basil or parsley instead of dill. Or add a tablespoon of tomato sauce or sun-dried tomatoes.

1 tbs. reduced calorie mayonnaise
2 tbs. nonfat yogurt
1 tbs. Dijon-style mustard
1 tbs. fresh dill weed or 1/2 tsp.dried
1 1/4 lb. fish fillets or steaks

Preheat broiler. In a small bowl, combine all ingredients except fish. Coat both sides of fish with mayonnaise mixture. Place fish on lightly greased broiler pan; broil on one side about 5 minutes. Turn and broil until fish is opaque.

Nutritional information per serving 167 calories, 15% calories from fat, 3 grams fat (3/4 tsp. fat), .5 grams saturated fat, 79 mg cholesterol, 33 grams protein, 1 gram carbohydrate, 188 mg sodium

Oriental Flavored Fish

Servings: 4

Using foil on the grill prevents sticking and makes clean-up easy.

1 (14½ ozs.) can pineapple chunks, no sugar added, drained, juice reserved
1-2 green onions, thinly sliced
¼ cup dry sherry
3 tbs. red wine vinegar
1 tbs. low-sodium soy sauce
½ tsp. grated fresh ginger
4 fish steaks (1¼ lbs. total)
2 tsp. safflower oil

In a shallow pan, combine pineapple juice, green onions, sherry, vinegar, soy sauce and ginger; add fish and marinate for 30 minutes. Prepare grill. Tear off a large piece of heavy duty foil, crimp edges and brush with oil. When coals are hot, place foil directly on grill. Remove fish from marinade and place on foil; add pineapple. Grill fish, basting with marinade. Cooking time will vary, but allow 13 minutes per inch of thickness.

Nutritional information per serving 237 calories, 26% calories from fat, 6 grams fat (1½ tsp. fat), .9 grams saturated fat, 59 mg cholesterol, 24 grams protein, 17 grams carbohydrate, 207 mg sodium

Pan "Fried" Fish

Servings: 4

Choose firm, thick fish fillets and a nonstick skillet when "frying" fish this lowfat way.

1 egg white
2 tsp. cornstarch
1⁄4 cup cornmeal
2 tsp. dry mustard
1⁄2 tsp. minced onion
1⁄2 tsp. garlic powder
1⁄2 tsp. salt-free seasoning blend
freshly ground pepper to taste
1 1⁄4 lbs. fish fillets
2 tsp. safflower or corn oil

In one bowl, combine egg white and cornstarch; mix well. In another bowl, blend cornmeal and seasonings. Dip fish in egg white mixture and then in cornmeal. Brush a nonstick skillet with 1 tsp. oil, heat and brown fish. Reduce heat, cover and cook fish for 5-7 minutes (time will depend on thickness of fish). Remove fish from pan and brush pan with oil. Brown other side of fish, reduce heat, cover and cook 5-7 minutes.

Nutritional information per serving 191 calories, 22% calories from fat, 4 grams fat (1 tsp. fat), .6 grams saturated fat, 61 mg cholesterol, 27 grams protein, 9 grams carbohydrate, 90 mg sodium

Dipping Sauce for "Fried" Fish

8 tablespoons

Something like tartar sauce, but without the fat! This is an example of a recipe with a high percentage of calories from fat, but the total calories and fat are so low, it is a very good alternative to other sauces.

1 tbs. reduced calorie mayonnaise
1/4 cup nonfat yogurt
1 tbs. chopped green onion
1 tbs. chopped parsley
1/2 tsp. dill weed
1 tsp. Dijon-style mustard

In a small bowl, combine all ingredients; serve with fish.

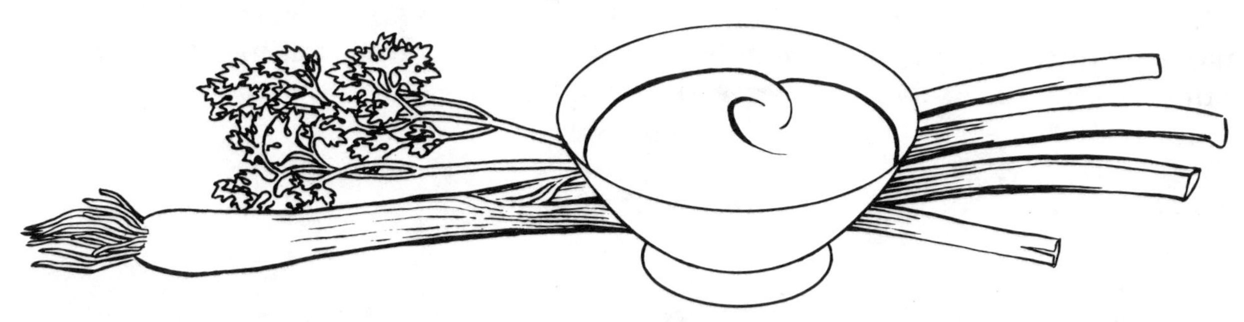

Nutritional information per tablespoon 11 calories, 54% calories from fat, 1 gram fat (1/4 tsp. fat), 0 grams saturated fat, 1 mg cholesterol, 0 grams protein, 1 gram carbohydrate, 25 mg sodium

Shrimp Salad

Servings: 4

For an attractive luncheon plate, serve a trio of salads: a tomato stuffed with shrimp salad, a fruit salad and a mixed green salad.

3/4 lb. small cooked shrimp
1/4 cup chopped celery
1/2 red bell pepper, chopped
2 green onions, thinly sliced
2 tbs. reduced calorie mayonnaise
4 tbs. nonfat yogurt
2-3 tbs. chopped fresh dill or
 2 tsp. dried
4 tomatoes
spinach leaves (optional)

In a medium bowl, combine shrimp, celery, pepper and onions. Blend mayonnaise, yogurt and dill; add to shrimp mixture. Scoop out centers of tomatoes. Stuff with shrimp salad and serve on spinach leaves if desired.

Nutritional information per serving 133 calories, 27% calories from fat, 4 grams fat (1 tsp. fat), .9 grams saturated fat, 132 mg cholesterol, 20 grams protein, 5 grams carbohydrate, 189 mg sodium

Tandori Shrimp

Servings: 4

The longer the shrimp marinate in this sauce the better, but if you forget to allow for a long marinating time, the shrimp will still taste good!

3/4 cup nonfat yogurt
2 tsp. grated fresh ginger
1-2 cloves garlic, minced or mashed
1 tsp. dry mustard
1 tbs. fresh lemon juice
1-2 tsp. curry powder
1/8 tsp. cayenne
1 lb. medium-sized shrimp, peeled, deveined

In a large bowl, combine yogurt, ginger, garlic, mustard, lemon juice and spices. Add shrimp; marinate several hours or overnight. Thread shrimp on skewers and grill or broil, about 3 to 5 minutes.

Nutritional information per serving 154 calories, 13% calories from fat, 2 grams fat (1/2 tsp. fat), .6 grams saturated fat, 173 mg cholesterol, 27 grams protein, 7 grams carbohydrate, 201 mg sodium

Grilled Scallops

Servings: 4

Wooden skewers might burst into flame on the grill unless you soak them in water before threading them with the fish and vegetables.

1 lb. sea scallops
2 tsp. olive oil
2 tbs. nonfat yogurt
1/4 tsp. dried crushed red pepper
1 tbs. coarse ground prepared mustard
1 tsp. dried rosemary
1/2 lb. cherry tomatoes

In a large bowl, combine scallops, oil, yogurt, seasonings and tomatoes. Thread scallops and tomatoes on skewers. Grill or broil for about 5 minutes.

Nutritional information per serving 139 calories, 22% calories from fat, 3 grams fat (3/4 tsp. fat), .5 grams saturated fat, 38 mg cholesterol, 21 grams protein, 6 grams carbohydrate, 242 mg sodium

Oriental Scallops

Servings: 2

Rice seems the obvious choice to go alongside this dish, but for something a little bit different, serve steamed Oriental noodles.

¾ lb. small bay scallops
1 green onion, chopped
1 tsp. grated fresh ginger
1 tbs. low-sodium soy sauce
1 tbs. sherry
1 tsp. olive oil
2 tsp. Dijon-style mustard
1 clove garlic, minced

In a small bowl, combine all ingredients and refrigerate for 20 minutes. Just before serving, heat a nonstick skillet. Add scallops with liquid; quickly cook, stirring, until they are no longer translucent, about 3 minutes. Serve over rice or steamed Oriental noodles.

Nutritional information per serving 192 calories, 19% calories from fat, 4 grams fat (1 tsp. fat), 1 gram saturated fat, 56 mg cholesterol, 31 grams protein, 6 grams carbohydrate, 595 mg sodium

Salmon Patties with Cucumber Sauce

Servings: 4

During World War II, canned salmon disappeared from the grocer's shelf. When salmon patties again appeared on the menu, we knew that normal times had returned.

1 (7½ ozs.) can salmon, drained, 2 tbs. liquid reserved
2 egg whites
juice of ½ lemon
2 tbs. grated onion
½ cup unsalted cracker crumbs or matzoh meal
1 tsp. dried dill weed
dash of Tabasco sauce
½ tsp. safflower oil
cucumber sauce

In a medium bowl, flake salmon with all ingredients except oil. Mix well and shape into patties. If mixture seems dry, add more liquid. Brush a heated non-stick skillet with oil. Add patties and cook until brown; turn and cook on other side. Serve with cucumber sauce.

Cucumber Sauce

1 cup nonfat yogurt
1 small cucumber, peeled, seeded, grated
1-2 green onions, thinly sliced
1 tsp. low-sodium soy sauce

In a small bowl, combine all ingredients, cover and chill.

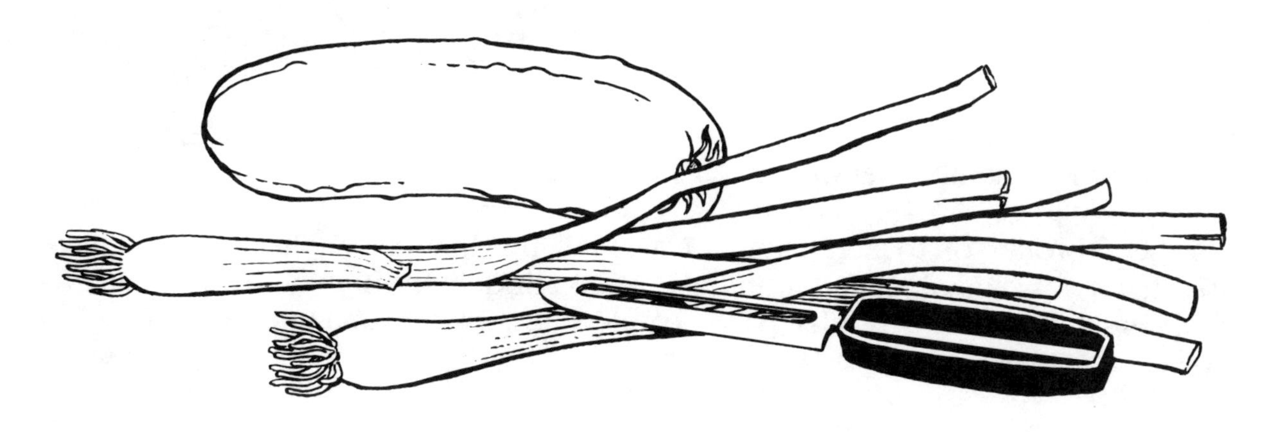

Nutritional information per serving with 1/4 cup sauce 159 calories, 32% calories from fat, 6 grams fat (1½ tsp. fat), .6 grams saturated fat, 34 mg cholesterol, 16 grams protein, 11 grams carbohydrate, 93 mg sodium

Tuna Puffs

Servings: 6

A quick lunch from foods kept on hand in pantry and freezer!

1 (7 ozs.) can water-packed tuna, drained
2 tbs. reduced calorie mayonnaise
½ cup nonfat yogurt
1 tsp. Dijon-style mustard
½ tsp. salt-free seasoning blend
1 tsp. lemon juice
1 green onion, chopped
3 whole wheat hamburger buns, split, toasted

Preheat broiler or toaster oven. In a small bowl, break up tuna with a fork. Stir in mayonnaise, yogurt, mustard, seasoning, lemon juice and onion. Arrange split buns on a broiler pan, cut side up. Divide tuna mix among 6 bun halves and broil for about 3 minutes.

Nutritional information per serving 135 calories, 21% calories from fat, 3 grams fat (¾ tsp. fat), 1 gram saturated fat, 21 mg cholesterol, 13 grams protein, 13 grams carbohydrate, 309 mg sodium

Vegetables

When we eat fewer meats and other foods high in fats, we must fill in the vacant spaces in our menus and our stomachs with something else. Let's eat more vegetables! Vegetables offer a tremendous variety of tastes, colors and textures, and a wealth of fiber, vitamins, minerals and carbohydrates. And vegetables are truly American foods. Almost half of the world's edible plants originated in the Americas. Long before white settlers arrived, Indians in the New World cultivated corn (maize), potatoes, beans, squashes, tomatoes, chili peppers and pumpkin.

Vegetables also have a role in disease prevention. Recent research seems to indicate that eating one of the cruciferous vegetables (cabbage, broccoli, Brussels sprouts, kohlrabi, cauliflower, kale, rutabaga and turnips) once a week may help to prevent certain kinds of cancer.

Like any other food, vegetables must be cooked properly to preserve their good qualities. Over-cooking destroys some nutrients, and dousing vegetables with fatty sauces turns them into high-caloric time bombs. A squeeze of lemon or a dash of flavored vinegar is all you need for tender-crisp steamed vegetables. When you want something more unusual, try one of our recipes.

Grilled Herb Marinated Vegetables

Servings: 2

Mushrooms and/or tomatoes could be added to these vegetable packets.

1 tbs. red wine vinegar
1 clove garlic, minced or mashed
1 tsp. Dijon-style mustard
1 tbs. minced fresh herbs such as thyme and rosemary, or 1 tsp. dried
2 tsp. olive oil
freshly ground pepper to taste
2-3 green onions, sliced
2 small zucchini, sliced
2 small red new potatoes, steamed until just tender
1 red, yellow or green bell pepper, quartered, seeded

In a large bowl, combine vinegar, garlic, mustard, spices and oil. Add vegetables and toss with dressing; marinate 30 minutes. Heat coals. Tear 2 pieces of foil large enough to hold vegetables. Divide vegetables and place in center of foil. Fold up edges of foil to make airtight packages. Place over hot coals and grill for 5 to 10 minutes.

Nutritional information per serving 124 calories, 34% calories from fat, 5 grams fat (1¼ tsp. fat), .7 grams saturated fat, 0 mg cholesterol, 3 grams protein, 19 grams carbohydrate, 41 mg sodium

Blazing Tomato Stir-Fry

Servings: 4

Eric Johnson and David Williams say that this vegetable dish is a favorite of college students who believe that food isn't properly seasoned unless it's painful to eat. If you concur, increase the amount of chili peppers and/or add serrano peppers. This recipe is for ordinary taste buds.

2 tsp. safflower oil
1 medium onion, chopped
2-3 cloves garlic, minced or mashed
1/4 tsp. dried crushed chili peppers
2 tbs. peanut butter, 100% peanuts, no salt added
1 (8 ozs.) can tomato sauce
4 cups chopped vegetables (broccoli, red pepper, celery, mushrooms or zucchini)
2 cups cooked brown or converted rice

Heat a nonstick skillet; add oil and cook onions, garlic and chili peppers until onions are soft. Add peanut butter and 2 tablespoons tomato sauce; stir-fry 2 to 3 minutes. Add vegetables and remaining tomato sauce; stir-fry 5 to 10 minutes. Vegetables should be tender-crisp. Stir in rice and heat until warm.

Nutritional information per serving 240 calories, 27% calories from fat, 7.5 grams fat (2 tsp. fat), 1 gram saturated fat, 0 mg cholesterol, 8 grams protein, 38 grams carbohydrate, 381 mg sodium

Red and Green Cabbage Slaw

Servings: 6

Save the outer shell of the red cabbage, crisp in ice water, drain and use as a salad bowl for the slaw.

1½ cups shredded red cabbage
1½ cups shredded green cabbage
1 carrot, grated
¼ cup grated onion
¼ cup reduced calorie mayonnaise
¼ cup nonfat yogurt
1 tsp. sugar
2 tbs. red wine vinegar
1 tsp. celery seed

In a salad bowl, combine cabbages, carrot and onion. In a small bowl, mix together remaining ingredients, add to vegetables and toss. Cover and let sit in the refrigerator several hours or overnight.

Nutritional information per serving 55 calories, 52% calories from fat, 3.5 grams fat (1 tsp. fat), .7 grams saturated fat, 4 mg cholesterol, 1 gram protein, 6 grams carbohydrate, 78 mg sodium

Brussels Sprouts with Walnuts

Servings: 4

To keep vegetables green, take the lid off the pot the first few minutes of cooking.

2 cups fresh Brussels sprouts
1 tsp. olive oil
2 green onions, finely chopped
2 tsp. finely chopped walnuts

In a saucepan, steam Brussels sprouts until tender. Set aside. In a nonstick skillet, heat oil. Add Brussels sprouts, onions and walnuts; stir-fry 2 to 3 minutes.

Nutritional information per serving 53 calories, 36% calories from fat, 2.7 grams fat (1/2 tsp. fat), .3 grams saturated fat, 0 mg cholesterol, 3 grams protein, 7 grams carbohydrate, 9 mg sodium

Orange Glazed Beets

Servings: 4

Beets are easier to peel after cooking. Steaming and baking are the preferred methods of cooking for this vegetable.

4 medium-sized cooked beets
½ cup frozen orange juice concentrate
2 tsp. grated orange zest (optional)
1 tsp. grated fresh ginger or ¼ tsp. dry
1½ tsp. cornstarch

Peel beets and slice. Set aside. In a saucepan, combine remaining ingredients and simmer 2 to 3 minutes. Add beets and cook until sauce thickens.

Nutritional information per serving 78 calories, 1% calories from fat, .1 grams fat (0 tsp. fat), 0 grams saturated fat, 0 mg cholesterol, 1 gram protein, 18 grams carbohydrate, 25 mg sodium

Fragrant Beet Greens

Servings: 4

Use young greens; the old ones are tough and have a strong flavor. If beet roots are less than ½" across, chop and toss into stir-fry.

2 tsp. sesame oil, divided
3-4 green onions, thinly sliced
1 tsp. grated fresh ginger
4-6 fresh mint leaves or 1 tsp. dried
3-4 cups coarsely chopped beet greens and roots
grated zest of 1 lemon (optional)
1 tbs. fresh lemon juice
1 tsp. sesame seeds

Heat a nonstick skillet; add 1 tsp. sesame oil, onions and ginger. Stir-fry 3 to 5 minutes. Add remaining oil, beet greens with beet root and mint; stir-fry 3 to 5 minutes. Add lemon zest and lemon juice. Sprinkle with sesame seeds and serve.

Nutritional information per serving 38 calories, 60% calories from fat, 2.7 grams fat (½ tsp. fat), .4 grams saturated fat, 0 mg cholesterol, 1 gram protein, 3 grams carbohydrate, 77 mg sodium

Peachy Squash

Servings: 4

Cooked sweet potatoes, either leftover or canned, can be substituted for the squash, especially if you're in a hurry. Assemble with other ingredients as directed and bake in a casserole.

1 large acorn squash
1 (1 lb.) can peaches in fruit juice
1/2 tsp. cinnamon
1 tbs. honey

Wash squash and stab in several places to allow steam to escape. Microwave on high for 15 minutes, turning once, or bake at 350° for 1 hour, until squash gives when pressed with a mittened hand. Drain canned peaches (save juice for other uses) and puree peaches in a food processor or blender. Cut squash in half and remove seeds. Scrape cooked pulp into food processor or a large bowl; save squash shell. Mix peaches, squash, cinnamon and honey. Return to shell or pour into a small casserole sprayed with nonstick coating. Return to oven or microwave to heat through before serving.

Nutritional information per serving 124 calories, 1% calories from fat, 0 grams fat (0 tsp. fat), 0 grams saturated fat, 0 mg cholesterol, 2 grams protein, 33 grams carbohydrate, 10 mg sodium

Baked Potatoes

Servings: 4

Potatoes have a reputation for being fattening because they hang out with the wrong crowd: butter, sour cream and cheese. These lowfat toppings will restore the potato's good name.

2 large baking potatoes

Preheat oven to 400°. Scrub potatoes thoroughly; pierce with a fork and bake for 1 hour. Cut potatoes in half. Scoop out pulp and mix with topping. Refill shell with potato mixture. Return to oven and heat for 2 to 3 minutes.

Southwest Potato Topping

1/4 cup nonfat milk
1 cup nonfat yogurt
2 tbs. reduced calorie mayonnaise
4 tbs. grated reduced fat cheese (less than 5 grams fat per oz.)
2 tsp. coarse ground prepared mustard
1 (4 ozs.) can chopped green chiles
1/4 tsp. dried crushed red pepper (optional)

In a medium bowl, combine all ingredients. Mix with potato pulp as directed.

Nutritional information per serving 212 calories, 17% calories from fat, 4 grams fat (1 tsp. fat), 2 grams saturated fat, 7 mg cholesterol, 9 grams protein, 36 grams carbohydrate, 590 mg sodium

Spinach Mushroom Potato Topping

1 tbs. olive oil
½ lb. mushrooms, sliced
1-2 cloves garlic, minced or mashed
1 (10 ozs.) pkg. frozen chopped spinach, well drained
½ cup lowfat ricotta cheese
½ cup nonfat milk
1 tsp. dry mustard
1 tbs. Dijon-style mustard

Heat a nonstick skillet; add oil. Add mushrooms and garlic; cook until mushrooms begin to brown. Add spinach and stir-fry 2 to 3 minutes. Mix in ricotta cheese, milk and mustard. Heat sauce 2 to 3 minutes. Mix with potato pulp as directed.

Nutritional information per serving 202 calories, 19% calories from fat, 4 grams fat (1 tsp. fat), 1 gram saturated fat, 6 mg cholesterol, 7 grams protein, 35 grams carbohydrate, 151 mg sodium

Old-Fashioned "French Fries"

Servings: 4

These oven "fried" potatoes are crisp on the outside and soft on the inside. The baking time depends on how thick you cut the potatoes.

4 baking potatoes
2 egg whites, lightly beaten
1 tsp. safflower oil
1 tbs. salt-free seasoning blend

Preheat oven to 450°. Slice potatoes lengthwise and then into ½" sticks. Dip potatoes into egg whites. Place potatoes on a nonstick baking sheet that has been brushed with oil. Sprinkle with seasoning. Bake for 15 to 20 minutes or until potatoes are brown and crisp, turning occasionally.

Nutritional information per serving 128 calories, 9% calories from fat, 1 gram fat (1/4 tsp. fat), .1 gram saturated fat, 0 mg cholesterol, 4 grams protein, 25 grams carbohydrate, 33 mg sodium

Candied Sweet Potatoes

Servings: 6

We like the combination of pineapple, orange and banana, but other juice concentrates may be used.

4-6 sweet potatoes or yams
2 kiwi fruits, peeled, sliced
½ cup frozen pineapple-orange-banana juice concentrate
¼ cup water

Preheat oven to 350°. Wash and scrub potatoes and bake until soft. Remove skin if desired and slice into ½" rounds. Place potato rounds in a shallow baking pan. Layer with kiwi. Combine juice concentrate and water; pour over potatoes and bake for 20 minutes.

Nutritional information per serving 104 calories, 2% calories from fat, .2 grams fat (0 tsp. fat), 0 grams saturated fat, 0 mg cholesterol, 2 grams protein, 25 grams carbohydrate, 10 mg sodium

Snacks and Party Food

What makes a snack satisfying? For many of us, it's the *crunch*. We like snappy chips and crackers that break with a nice crackling sound. Some of these snacks can also be low in fat. Toasted corn tortillas (dipped in salsa), crackers and pretzels made without fat, crispy shredded wheat cereal or popcorn can all be lowfat or fat-free, providing that you read the labels carefully so that you choose lowfat products, and then don't add oil or butter or cheese or other kinds of fat to your munchies.

Fresh vegetables cut and ready in the refrigerator will also satisfy that urge to crunch. Our recipes will give you quick alternatives to high-fat packaged dips.

A sweet tooth doesn't always need to be sated with candies that are high in fat. Avoid chocolates, chocolate-coated and creamy candies. Instead, choose hard candies and dried fruits to eat out of hand, or buy good quality jams and preserves to eat on plain toast or English muffins.

Party food and snacks can creep up on you. Each small tidbit may be low in fat and calories, but if you nibble away all evening, your total intake will be shockingly high!

Better Spreads and Dips

These spreads will keep in the refrigerator for about 5 days. Use toasted pita bread, oven-crisped tortillas or vegetables as dippers. Stuff cherry tomatoes, mushrooms or celery with spreads. For each recipe, combine all ingredients in the bowl of a blender or food processor and process until smooth. Cover and refrigerate. For a thinner dip, increase the yogurt. To make a thicker dip, use yogurt cheese instead of plain yogurt in any of these recipes. Place nonfat yogurt (any brand that does not contain gelatin) in a strainer lined with a cheese cloth or a coffee filter. Set in a bowl and refrigerate for 4 to 6 hours. The thick yogurt that remains is yogurt cheese.

Spinach Spread

16 tablespoons

½ cup 1% fat cottage cheese
½ cup nonfat yogurt
½ cup washed fresh spinach, finely chopped, or frozen spinach, drained
1-2 green onions, chopped
½ tsp. curry powder, or to taste
1 tsp. toasted sesame seeds
freshly ground pepper to taste

Nutritional information per tablespoon 11 calories, 16% calories from fat, .2 grams fat (0 tsp. fat), 0 grams saturated fat, .5 mg cholesterol, 1 gram protein, 1 gram carbohydrate, 36 mg sodium

Cheesy Tomato Dip

16 tablespoons

1 cup plain nonfat yogurt
2 tbs. Dijon-style mustard
2 tbs. grated Parmesan cheese
2 tbs. chopped tomato
1 tbs. chopped fresh basil or ½ tsp. dried

Nutritional information per tablespoon 13 calories, 22% calories from fat, .3 grams fat (0 tsp. fat), 0 grams saturated fat, .7 mg cholesterol, 1 gram protein, 1 gram carbohydrate, 47 mg sodium

Blue Yogurt Dip

16 tablespoons

2 tbs. crumbled blue cheese
1 tsp. minced dry onion
1 cup plain nonfat yogurt

Nutritional information per tablespoon 11 calories, 22% calories from fat, .3 grams fat (0 tsp. fat), .2 grams saturated fat, .9 mg cholesterol, 1 gram protein, 1 gram carbohydrate, 23 mg sodium

Salmon Spread

16 tablespoons

1 (7.5 ozs.) can salmon, drained
1 tsp. grated onion
½ tsp. dried dill weed
drop Tabasco sauce
½ cup nonfat yogurt

Nutritional information per tablespoon 26 calories, 30% calories from fat, .8 grams fat (¼ tsp. fat), .1 gram saturated fat, 9 mg cholesterol, 3 grams protein, 1 gram carbohydrate, 16 mg sodium

Baked Garlic

Servings: 4

The whiff of garlic roasting is a delight to the senses. Purchase large, firm bulbs for this dish.

1 or 2 whole fresh garlic bulbs (about ½ lb.)

Preheat oven to 350°. Wrap garlic in aluminum foil and bake for about 1 hour or until garlic is soft. Time will depend on size. To serve: cut tips of cloves and place whole bulb on a serving tray. Surround with fresh bread, good flavored mustard and chopped oil-packed sun-dried tomatoes. Guests help themselves by breaking off cloves and squeezing garlic on bread which has been spread with mustard and tomatoes. Or scoop garlic out with the tip of a knife or a small spoon.

Nutritional information per serving of garlic only 122 calories, 3% calories from fat, .4 grams fat (0 tsp. fat), 0 grams saturated fat, 0 mg cholesterol, 5 grams protein, 27 grams carbohydrate, 14 mg sodium

Miniature Tostada

24 tostadas

Toasted pita triangles are the base for these bite-sized tostadas.

1 cup cooked kidney beans
2 tsp. Dijon-style mustard
2 tsp. chili powder
1/2 tsp. *each* onion powder and garlic powder or flakes
1/4 cup salsa
2 whole pita breads
1/4 cup sliced green onions or bean sprouts
2 tbs. grated reduced fat cheese (less than 5 grams per oz.)

Preheat oven to 350°. In a small saucepan, combine beans, mustard, seasoning and salsa; mash with a fork. Simmer for 5 minutes. Meanwhile, split pita bread, cut each round into 6 triangles, and toast on a cookie sheet in oven. Place 1 tbs. bean spread on each toasted pita triangle. Top each with onions and cheese. Return to oven until cheese melts. Recipe can be doubled.

Nutritional information per tostada 28 calories, 10% calories from fat, .3 grams fat (0 tsp. fat), 0 grams saturated fat, .3 mg cholesterol, 1 gram protein, 5 grams carbohydrate, 42 mg sodium

Smoky Eggplant

16 tablespoons

Our eggplant tastes best when done on the grill, but it can be charred under the broiler. We serve it on a bed of spinach surrounded by cherry tomatoes and strips of red or yellow bell peppers.

1 large eggplant, or 2 small ones
2 tbs. lime juice
1-2 garlic cloves, mashed
2 tbs. toasted sesame seeds
2 tbs. chopped fresh parsley or 2 tbs. pomegranate seeds

Pierce eggplants a few times to allow steam to escape. Place on a preheated grill or under broiler. Broil until skins are charred and eggplant collapses, turning to get all sides, about 35 minutes depending on size of eggplant. Cool. Peel eggplant. In a blender or food processor, combine pulp with all ingredients except parsley and puree until smooth. Garnish with parsley.

Nutritional information per tablespoon 10 calories, 46% calories from fat, .6 gram fat (1/8 tsp. fat), 0 grams saturated fat, 0 mg cholesterol, 0 grams protein, 1 gram carbohydrate, .7 mg sodium

Broiled Stuffed Mushrooms

15 mushrooms

For a more formal dinner party, present stuffed mushrooms at the table for the first course, serving three to a plate. At an informal party, serve them with toothpicks and napkins.

1 lb. large mushrooms
3 tbs. dry sherry
1 small onion, chopped
3-4 sprigs fresh parsley, chopped
3/4 cup soft bread crumbs
1/2 cup finely minced cooked chicken
1/2 tsp. *each* dried marjoram and dried basil
freshly ground pepper to taste

Rinse mushrooms and wipe dry. Remove and chop stems. Place caps on a large baking sheet. In a large skillet, heat 1 tbs. sherry; add onion, parsley and chopped mushroom stems. Cook for 2 to 3 minutes. Stir in remaining sherry and other ingredients. Continue to cook for 1 minute. Stuff mushrooms with this filling. Cover mushrooms with a damp paper towel and refrigerate until serving time. Then broil under a preheated broiler for 3 to 5 minutes until lightly browned. Serve hot.

Nutritional information per mushroom 30 calories, 19% calories from fat, 1 gram fat (1/4 tsp. fat), 0 grams saturated fat, 4 mg cholesterol, 2 grams protein, 3 grams carbohydrate, 17 mg sodium

Crunchy Onion Rings

Servings: 4

Oven "frying" gives a crisp coating without all the fat. This technique will work with any vegetable.

2 tsp. safflower oil
2 large onions
2 tbs. all-purpose flour
2 egg whites
2 tbs. nonfat milk
1 tbs. cornstarch
3/4 cup panko (Japanese bread crumbs) or plain bread crumbs
1 tsp. salt-free seasoning blend

Preheat oven to 400°. Brush oil on 2 nonstick pans and set aside. Slice onions and separate rings; set aside. Place flour in a paper bag. In a shallow bowl, combine egg whites, milk and cornstarch. In another paper bag, combine panko and seasoning. Shake rings in flour; shake off excess. Dip rings in egg mixture and then shake in bread crumbs. Place rings on pans and bake for 10 to 15 minutes; turn and bake until onion rings are crisp.

Nutritional information per serving 102 calories, 25% calories from fat, 3 grams fat (3/4 tsp. fat), .4 grams saturated fat, 0 mg cholesterol, 4 grams protein, 15 grams carbohydrate, 74 mg sodium

Crispy Wonton

40 wonton

We like to make a large quantity of these spicy morsels and freeze them for future use. If you're making fewer wonton, use the extra filling to top a baked potato.

1 (10 ozs.) pkg. frozen chopped spinach, thawed
5 tsp. sesame oil
½ cup finely chopped onion
1 tsp. dry mustard
1 tsp. dried rosemary leaves
freshly grated nutmeg to taste
½ cup lowfat ricotta cheese
2 tsp. low-sodium soy sauce
2 pkgs. wonton wrappers (20-24 per pkg.)

Preheat oven to 400°. Drain spinach and squeeze dry. Heat a nonstick skillet; add 1 tsp. oil. Add onion and cook until soft and golden. Add spinach and seasonings; cook over low heat for 10-15 minutes or until mixture is dry. Stir in ricotta cheese and soy sauce. Place a teaspoon of filling on each wonton skin; fold over once to make a triangle, moistening edges with water to seal. Rub each package with a drop or two of the remaining oil (this is best done with fingers). Place on a nonstick cookie sheet and bake for 20 minutes. If you freeze unbaked wonton, it is not necessary to thaw before baking.

Nutritional information per serving 36 calories, 15% calories from fat, 1 gram fat (¼ tsp. fat), 0 grams saturated fat, .5 mg cholesterol, 1 gram protein, 7 grams carbohydrate, 34 mg sodium

Steamed Clams in Wine Broth

Servings: 6

A loaf of warm French bread is a perfect accompaniment to this elegant appetizer.

1 tbs. olive oil
2 green onions, thinly sliced
2-3 cloves garlic, minced or mashed
1 tbs. Dijon-style mustard
1/4 tsp. dried dill weed
1/8 tsp. cayenne
1 cup dry white wine
2 lbs. clams in the shell, scrubbed clean

Heat a large saucepan; add oil. Add onions and garlic and cook until soft. Add remaining ingredients except clams. Bring to a boil, reduce heat and simmer 5 minutes. Add clams, bring back to a boil, cover and steam over medium-high heat for 5 to 7 minutes or until clams have opened.

Nutritional information per serving 97 calories, 32% calories from fat, 3 grams fat (3/4 tsp. fat), .4 grams saturated fat, 33 mg cholesterol, 13 grams protein, 3 grams carbohydrate, 89 mg sodium

Oat Bran Treats

20 oat balls

Making these no-bake cookies is an easy way to add fiber to your diet.

1⁄2 cup chopped dried apples
1⁄4 cup raisins
1⁄2-3⁄4 cup apple juice or cider
1 cup oat bran
1⁄4 cup nonfat dry milk powder

In a blender or food processor, combine dried apples, raisins and 1⁄2 cup apple juice; puree. Add oat bran and dry milk; mix well. If mixture is dry, add more juice. Roll dough into balls about the size of a walnut. Let stand 20 minutes.

Nutritional information per serving 28 calories, 6% calories from fat, .3 grams fat (0 tsp. fat), 0 grams saturated fat, 0 mg cholesterol, 1 gram protein, 7 grams carbohydrate, 6 mg sodium

Desserts

None of us wants to give up dessert, and with a little careful planning we shouldn't have to. Fruit, either fresh, frozen or canned with no sugar added, is always a good choice. When one fruit gets monotonous, create new dishes by combining them in new ways: bananas with kiwi and blueberries; strawberries with mandarin oranges; canned pineapple with apples and raisins; or pears with red grapes.

But on those occasions when you want something special, fruit may not be enough. The recipes we offer are our versions of some traditional favorites that have been adapted to new standards. We have cut out butter, cream and whole eggs, and substituted ingredients that have much less saturated fat and cholesterol. One thing we haven't cut down on is the good, rich flavor that we all like for dessert.

Here's where portion size and menu-planning are really important. Although our recipes have lots less fat than the originals, they still contain some fat. So if you serve a rich dessert like ***A BETTER Better-than-Sex Cake,*** choose a main dish that has a minimum of fat in it, like ***Oriental Scallops*** or ***Quick Broiled Fish,*** to keep your total intake of fat under 20 grams.

Pumpkin Pie

Servings: 8

No one will ever know that this is a lowfat dessert. The evaporated skim milk is the secret.

3 egg whites, slightly beaten or imitation egg equal to 2 eggs
1 (16 ozs.) can pumpkin
1⁄2 cup sugar
1⁄4 cup instant nonfat dry milk powder
1 tsp. cinnamon
1⁄4 tsp. freshly grated nutmeg
1 1⁄2 cups undiluted evaporated skim milk
1 unbaked ***Pie Crust Made with Oil,*** page 136

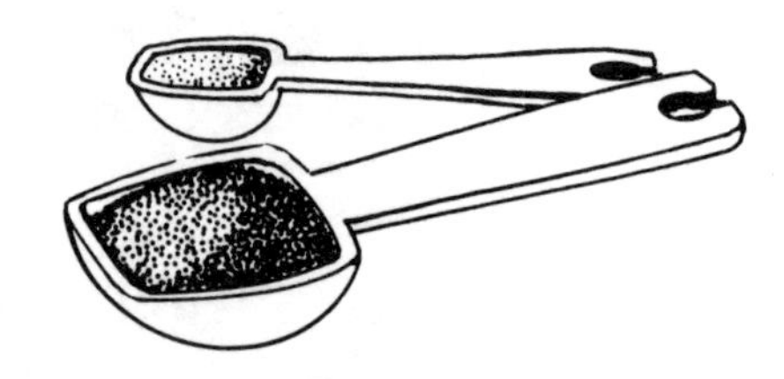

Prepare crust. Preheat oven to 425°. In a large mixing bowl, combine all ingredients; pour into pie shell. Bake 15 minutes; reduce temperature to 350° and bake 40 to 45 minutes or until a knife inserted near the center comes out clean.

Nutritional information per serving 221 calories, 22% calories from fat, 6 grams fat (1 1⁄2 tsp. fat), .6 grams saturated fat, 2 mg cholesterol, 8 grams protein, 36 grams carbohydrate, 89 mg sodium

Chocolate Pie

Servings: 8

Choco-holics rejoice! A square of baking chocolate contains 15 grams of fat, but substituting 3 tbs. of cocoa gives you only 2 grams of fat.

1/4 cup sugar
1/4 cup unsweetened cocoa
1 cup lowfat ricotta cheese
1/2 cup nonfat milk
1 tsp. vanilla
1 tbs. coffee-flavored liqueur or 1 tsp. instant espresso powder
dissolved in 1 tbs. hot water
1 ***Crumb Crust,*** page 137

In a food processor or blender, combine sugar, cocoa, ricotta cheese, milk and vanilla; puree until smooth. Pour chocolate mixture into a small saucepan. Simmer until thick, stirring constantly for about 5 minutes. Stir in liqueur. Pour chocolate mixture into crust and refrigerate until set.

Nutritional information per serving 141 calories, 29% calories from fat, 5 grams fat (1 1/4 tsp. fat), .9 grams saturated fat, 5 mg cholesterol, 4 grams protein, 22 grams carbohydrate, 187 mg sodium

Chocolate Pie with Strawberry Topping

Servings: 8

Fresh strawberries and chocolate are a delicious combination.

1 ***Chocolate Pie,*** page 131
1 pint whole strawberries
3 tbs. orange marmalade, made without sugar
1 tbs. coffee-flavored liqueur or rum

Wash and dry berries; remove stems and set aside. In a small saucepan, combine orange marmalade and liqueur; heat until glaze is thin. Dip berries in glaze and place on pie, tip side up. Refrigerate until served.

Nutritional information per serving 168 calories, 25% calories from fat, 5 grams fat (1¼ tsp. fat), .9 grams saturated fat, 5 mg cholesterol, 4 grams protein, 28 grams carbohydrate, 189 mg sodium

Lemon Ricotta Cheese Pie

Servings: 8

The tang of fresh lemon makes this pie a favorite.

1½ cups whole wheat bread crumbs (about 3 slices)
1 tbs. polyunsaturated margarine, melted
1 tsp. sugar
zest of ¼ lemon
¾ cup sugar
2 cups lowfat ricotta cheese
1 cup plain nonfat yogurt
3 egg whites
1 tbs. cornstarch
3 tbs. fresh lemon juice
½ tsp. vanilla

Preheat oven to 350°. In a medium bowl, combine bread crumbs, margarine and 1 tsp. sugar. Press mixture into the bottom and sides of a 9" pie pan. Bake for 8-10 minutes. In a blender or food processor, process lemon zest and sugar until lemon is finely chopped. Transfer to a small bowl and set aside. Process ricotta cheese in blender until creamy and smooth. Add yogurt and egg whites; process until well-mixed. Sprinkle lemon-sugar mixture and cornstarch over cheese; blend until smooth. Blend in lemon juice and vanilla. Pour cheese mixture into baked crumb crust. Bake for 1 hour or until firm when lightly touched in the center. Cool pie in open oven for 2 hours. Chill. Pie will fall.

Nutritional information per serving 170 calories, 15% calories from fat, 3 grams fat (¾ tsp. fat), 1 gram saturated fat, 10 mg cholesterol, 7 grams protein, 30 grams carbohydrate, 250 mg sodium

Ricotta Almond Cheesecake

Servings: 8

Using lowfat ricotta cheese and nonfat yogurt instead of cream cheese and sour cream cuts 90% of the fat usually found in cheesecake!

1/4 cup sliced almonds
1 cup whole wheat bread crumbs (about 2 slices)
1 tbs. polyunsaturated margarine, melted
2 cups lowfat ricotta cheese
1 cup plain nonfat yogurt
3 egg whites, or imitation egg equivalent to 2 eggs
3/4 cup sugar
1 tbs. cornstarch
1 tsp. vanilla
1/2 tsp. almond extract

Preheat oven to 350°. Set aside 1 tbs. of almonds for garnish. Put remaining almonds in a blender or food processor, and process to fine crumbs. Combine almonds, bread crumbs and margarine. Press mix into bottom and sides of a 9" pie pan. Bake for 8 to 10 minutes.

In a blender or food processor, process ricotta cheese until creamy and smooth. Add yogurt and egg whites and process until well-mixed. Sprinkle sugar and cornstarch over cheese; blend until smooth. Blend in vanilla and almond extract and pour cheese mixture into crust. Scatter reserved almonds on top and bake for 1 hour or until firm when lightly touched in the center. Cool cheesecake in oven with door open for 2 hours. Chill. It is normal for cake to fall.

Nutritional information per serving 176 calories, 22% calories from fat, 4 grams fat (1 tsp. fat), 1 gram saturated fat, 10 mg cholesterol, 7 grams protein, 28 grams carbohydrate, 228 mg sodium

Pie Crust Made with Oil

Servings: 8

Traditional pie crust made with solid shortening yields 199 calories and 13 grams of fat (of which 3 grams are saturated fat) per serving. That's without filling. Our oil crust cuts those numbers by more than half.

1 cup all-purpose flour
2 tbs. safflower oil
4 tbs. ice water

Sift flour into a small bowl. Combine oil and water in one cup, but do not stir. Add all at once to flour and mix with a fork until a ball forms. Chill for easier handling. Roll out between sheets of waxed paper. Peel off top paper, turn and fit into pie pan. Remove second paper. Proceed with recipe for pie.

For a baked crust:

Prick bottom and sides with a fork. Bake at 450° for 10 to 12 minutes, or until golden.

Nutritional information per serving 87 calories, 37% calories from fat, 4 grams fat (1 tsp. fat), .3 grams saturated fat, 0 mg cholesterol, 2 grams protein, 12 grams carbohydrate, 0 mg sodium

Crumb Crust

Servings: 8

Some pies taste best with a crunchy crumb crust. Use your own filling recipes with our crusts made of whole wheat bread crumbs or graham crackers that don't contain animal fats or palm or coconut oils.

2 slices whole wheat bread, or 9 graham cracker squares
1 tbs. polyunsaturated margarine, melted
1 tsp. sugar

Preheat oven to 350°. In a food processor or blender, process bread or crackers to fine crumbs. Combine crumbs, margarine and sugar. Pat into bottom and sides of an 8"-9" pie pan. Bake for 8 to 10 minutes.

Nutritional information per serving (with bread crumbs) 32 calories, 46% calories from fat, 2 grams fat (½ tsp. fat), .4 gram saturated fat, 0 mg cholesterol, 1 gram protein, 4 grams carbohydrate, 62 mg sodium

Nutritional information per serving (with graham crackers) 82 calories, 39% calories from fat, 4 grams fat (1 tsp. fat), .3 grams saturated fat, 0 mg cholesterol, 1 gram protein, 12 grams carbohydrate, 113 mg sodium

Cockeyed Chocolate Cake

Servings: 9

Now we stir this old family stand-by in a bowl. When we were kids, we mixed this cake in its own baking pan so we wouldn't have any bowls to wash!

1½ cups sifted all-purpose flour
1 cup sugar
3 tbs. unsweetened cocoa
1 tsp. baking soda
5 tbs. safflower or corn oil
1 tbs. cider or white vinegar
1 tsp. vanilla
1 cup cold water

Preheat oven to 350°. In a medium bowl, sift together flour, sugar, cocoa and soda. Add oil, vinegar, vanilla and cold water. Stir until flour disappears. Pour into a lightly greased or nonstick 9"x9" square pan and bake for 25 to 30 minutes.

Nutritional information per serving 206 calories, 22% calories from fat, 5 grams fat (1¼ tsp. fat), 1 gram saturated fat, 0 mg cholesterol, 2 grams protein, 39 grams carbohydrate, 93 mg sodium

Claire's Carrot Cake

Servings: 16

Claire bakes this dense, fruitcake-like confection for her father, who tries to avoid fats but "gets awfully tired of angel food cakes."

2 cups grated carrots
1 cup dried currants or raisins
1 cup brown sugar
1½ cups water
2 tbs. safflower oil
1 cup all-purpose flour
1 cup whole wheat flour
3 tsp. pumpkin pie spices, or substitute ½ tsp. *each* ground cloves, allspice, nutmeg and 1 tsp. ground cinnamon
1½ tsp. baking soda
1 tsp. vanilla
½ cup walnuts, chopped

Preheat oven to 350°. Grease or spray a 9" square pan. In a saucepan, combine carrots, currants, brown sugar, water and oil; bring to a boil, reduce heat and simmer 5 minutes. Remove from heat. Combine flours, spices and soda and stir into carrot mixture. Stir in vanilla and nuts. Pour into prepared pan and bake 35 minutes or until a toothpick inserted into the center comes out clean.

Nutritional information per serving 182 calories, 21% calories from fat, 4 grams fat (1 tsp. fat), 0 grams saturated fat, 0 mg cholesterol, 3 grams protein, 35 grams carbohydrate, 90 mg sodium

A BETTER Better-Than-Sex Cake

Servings: 16

Where did this cake get started? We don't know, but the original version provided 405 calories (57% from fat), 26 grams of fat and 59 mg of cholesterol per serving. We developed our version at the request of Carol Garzona of the Hope Heart Institute.

1 cup dried currants or raisins
1 cup chocolate chips
1/2 cup chopped walnuts
1 tbs. cornstarch
1 box Duncan Hines Devil's Food cake mix*
imitation eggs equal to 4 eggs
3/4 cup unsweetened applesauce
1 cup plain nonfat yogurt
1 tsp. vanilla

Preheat oven to 350°. Lightly grease a 12-cup bundt pan and dust lightly with flour. In a small bowl, combine currants, chips, walnuts and cornstarch; stir to coat and set aside. In a large mixer bowl, combine remaining ingredients and mix on slow until blended. Then mix on medium for 2 minutes. Fold in currants and nuts until no white shows. Turn into prepared pan and bake 50 to 60 minutes until cake shrinks back from sides and top springs back when touched lightly. Cool in pan 25 minutes; finish cooling on a wire rack.

Frosting

We think this cake is great without frosting, but if you prefer, drizzle with a glaze made of 2 cups confectioner's sugar, ½ tsp. vanilla and enough nonfat milk for spreading consistency.

*Duncan Hines brand of cake mix is the only one we've found so far that does not contain animal fats or tropical fats (palm and coconut oils).

Nutritional information per serving without glaze 270 calories, 33% calories from fat, 10 grams fat (2½ tsp. fat), 3 grams saturated fat, 0 mg cholesterol, 5 grams protein, 41 grams carbohydrate, 304 mg sodium

Angel Food Cake

Servings: 8

Angel food cake is a great choice for lowfat diets, because it contains hardly any fat. Eat it plain or layer it with our chocolate frosting or with fruited nonfat yogurt *(see pages 143 and 144).*

½ cup sifted cake flour (or ½ cup minus 2 tbs. all-purpose flour)
¼ cup sugar
5 egg whites
½ tsp. cream of tartar
½ tsp. orange extract
1 tsp. vanilla
¼ cup orange juice concentrate, thawed, at room temperature

Preheat oven to 375°. Sift flour with sugar 4 times. In a large mixer bowl, beat egg whites until foamy; add cream of tartar. Beat until moist and glossy. In a cup, combine extracts with juice; slowly pour into egg whites. Continue beating until egg whites form soft, shiny peaks. In 3 additions, sift flour over egg white mixture and fold in. Pour into an ungreased 8" or 9" loaf pan and smooth batter into corners. Bake 25 minutes or until cake springs back when touched lightly. Cool upside down for 1 hour. Transfer to a wire rack.

Nutritional information per serving 70 calories, 1% calories from fat, 1 gram fat (¼ tsp. fat), 0 grams saturated fat, 0 mg cholesterol, 3 grams protein, 15 grams carbohydrate, 32 mg sodium

Angel Food Cake Layered with Chocolate Frosting

Servings: 8

Our yummy thick frosting can also be served with fruit as an elegant dessert.

2 tbs. unsweetened cocoa powder
2 tbs. sugar
2 tbs. orange juice concentrate, thawed or 1 tbs. orange-flavored liqueur
1/2 cup lowfat ricotta cheese
1/2 tsp. vanilla
1 ***Angel Food Cake***, page 142

In a small bowl, combine cocoa, sugar, juice concentrate and extract. Stir until smooth. In a food processor or blender, process cheese until smooth. Add cocoa and process until blended. Split cake into 3 horizontal layers; top each with chocolate mix and stack. This recipe makes about 3/4 cup of frosting. It can also be prepared with an electric beater or by hand, but it will have a grainy quality.

Nutritional information per serving 100 calories, 5% calories from fat, 1 gram fat (1/4 tsp. fat), 0 grams saturated fat, 2 mg cholesterol, 4 grams protein, 21 grams carbohydrate, 65 mg sodium

Strawberry Trifle

Servings: 8

Another variation on the angel food cake theme. Too busy to bake? Buy a plain angel food cake from a bakery.

2 cups sliced fresh strawberries
2 tbs. orange juice concentrate, thawed
1 tbs orange-flavored liqueur
2 tbs. brown sugar, divided
1 cup peach or other fruited nonfat yogurt
1 ***Angel Food Cake***, page 142

In a medium bowl, combine strawberries, juice concentrate, liqueur and 1 tbs. brown sugar. In a small bowl, combine yogurt with remaining brown sugar. Slice cake horizontally into 3 layers. Cover a layer with 1/3 strawberries and then 1/3 yogurt. Repeat with second and third layers. Chill overnight or for 10 hours before serving. For a more traditional trifle, arrange cake slices in a glass bowl and cover with fruit and yogurt.

Nutritional information per serving 158 calories, 3% calories from fat, 0 grams fat (0 tsp. fat), 0 grams saturated fat, 1 mg cholesterol, 7 grams protein, 32 grams carbohydrate, 78 mg sodium

Valentine Mousse

Servings: 4

What could send a more caring message than an attractive and delicious edible valentine that won't tax your lover's heart?

2-2½ cups unsweetened strawberries, fresh or frozen, thawed
4 tbs. juice concentrate (not pineapple)
2 tbs. sugar
1 envelope unflavored gelatin
1 cup lowfat ricotta cheese
2 tbs. orange-flavored liqueur or 2 tbs. low sugar orange marmalade

Set aside 6 perfect strawberries for garnish. In a food processor or blender, puree remaining strawberries, 3 tbs. juice concentrate and sugar. In a small saucepan, soften gelatin in ¼ cup of the puree. Stir over low heat until gelatin dissolves. Pour warm puree-gelatin mixture back into original puree in food processor and process briefly. Chill until slightly thickened. In a small bowl, whip ½ cup ricotta cheese until fluffy; stir in liqueur. Fold into gelatin mixture, pour into a heart-shaped mold and chill until firm, about 1 hour. To serve, unmold mousse on a serving plate. In a small bowl, whip remaining ½ cup cheese with remaining 1 tbs. juice concentrate. Mound whipped cheese on top of mousse and garnish with reserved whole berries.

Nutritional information per serving 150 calories, 7% calories from fat, 1 gram fat (1/4 tsp. fat), 1 gram saturated fat, 10 mg cholesterol, 5 grams protein, 28 grams carbohydrate, 135 mg sodium

Judy's Apple Crisp for a Crowd

Servings: 15

If your favorite apples aren't available, improve the ones you have by sprinkling sugar over apples that are too tart and lemon juice over those that are too sweet or lacking in flavor.

6-8 pie apples, sliced
1⁄4 cup polyunsaturated margarine
1⁄3 cup honey
2 1⁄2 cups rolled oats
3⁄4 cup all-purpose flour
1⁄2 cup finely chopped walnuts
1 1⁄2 tsp. pumpkin pie spice, or 1⁄2 tsp. *each* cinnamon, allspice, nutmeg
1 cup orange juice

Preheat oven to 375°. Arrange apples in a nonstick 11"x15" jelly roll pan (or spray with nonstick coating). In a saucepan, melt margarine and honey together. Stir in oats, flour, walnuts and spices. Spread over apple slices. Drizzle orange juice over all. Bake 40-45 minutes, until apples are soft and top is golden brown. If you wish, serve with a dollop of nonfat yogurt on top, sweetened with orange juice concentrate and/or candied ginger.

Nutritional information per serving without topping 170 calories, 21% calories from fat, 4 grams fat (1 tsp. fat), 1 gram saturated fat, 0 mg cholesterol, 3 grams protein, 32 grams carbohydrate, 27 mg sodium

Poached Pears with Berry Sauce

Servings: 4

Top each pear with lowfat ricotta cheese that has been flavored with poaching liquid.

2 medium-sized firm pears, halved, cored
1 cup pineapple juice
1/2 cup water
1 tsp. fresh lemon juice
1 tsp. vanilla
1 cup fresh or frozen raspberries
1 tbs. orange-flavored liqueur, or 1 tsp. orange extract
2 tbs. pineapple juice concentrate

Place pears in a pan large enough to hold them without touching. In a small bowl, combine pineapple juice, water, lemon juice and vanilla; pour over pears. Simmer covered for 15 minutes or until pears are soft but not mushy. Remove pears to a serving platter or individual bowls. Reduce syrup over high heat. Spoon over pears. Puree berries with liqueur and juice concentrate. At serving time, spoon berry sauce over pears. Top with ricotta cheese if desired.

Nutritional information per serving without topping 243 calories, 2% calories from fat, .5 grams fat (0 tsp. fat), 0 grams saturated fat, 0 mg cholesterol, 1 gram protein, 59 grams carbohydrate, 6 mg sodium

Rice Pudding

Servings: 6

Almonds and raisins were the traditional flavorings of the rice puddings of our childhood.

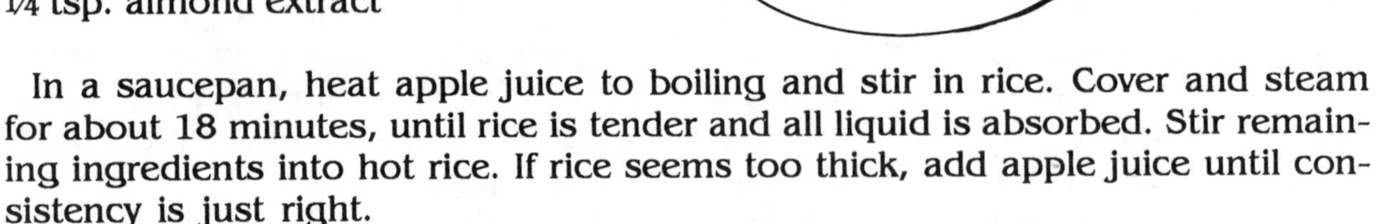

2 cups apple juice
1 cup converted rice
1⁄3 cup dry currants or raisins
2 tbs. honey
1⁄4 cup sliced almonds
1⁄4 tsp. almond extract

In a saucepan, heat apple juice to boiling and stir in rice. Cover and steam for about 18 minutes, until rice is tender and all liquid is absorbed. Stir remaining ingredients into hot rice. If rice seems too thick, add apple juice until consistency is just right.

Nutritional information per serving 224 calories, 9% calories from fat, 2 grams fat (1⁄2 tsp. fat), 0 grams saturated fat, 0 mg cholesterol, 3 grams protein, 48 grams carbohydrate, 7 mg sodium

Appendix

Dietary Recommendations from Diet and Health: Implications for Reducing Chronic Disease Risk, National Research Council

- Reduce total fat intake to 30% or less of calories. Reduce saturated fatty acid intake to less than 10% of calories, and the intake of cholesterol to less than 300 mg daily. The intake of fat and cholesterol can be reduced by substituting fish, poultry without skin, lean meats and low- or nonfat dairy products for fatty meats and whole-milk dairy products; by choosing more vegetables, fruits, cereals and legumes; and by limiting oils, fats, egg yolks, and fried and other fatty foods.
- Every day eat five or more servings of a combination of vegetables and fruits, especially green and yellow vegetables and citrus fruits. Also, increase intake of starches and other complex carbohydrates by eating six or more daily servings of a combination of breads, cereals and legumes.
- Maintain protein intake at moderate levels.
- Balance food intake and physical activity to maintain appropriate body weight.

- The committee does not recommend alcohol consumption. For those who drink alcoholic beverages, the committee recommends limiting consumption to the equivalent of less than one ounce of pure alcohol in a single day. This is the equivalent of two cans of beer, two small glasses of wine or two average cocktails. Pregnant women should avoid alcoholic beverages.
- Limit total daily intake of salt (sodium chloride) to 6 grams or less. Limit the use of salt in cooking and avoid adding it to food at the table. Salty, highly processed salty, salt-preserved and salt-pickled foods should be consumed sparingly.
- Maintain adequate calcium intake.
- Avoid taking dietary supplements in excess of the RDA (recommended dietary allowance) in any one day.
- Maintain an optimal intake of flouride, particularly during the years of primary and secondary tooth formation and growth.

Index

METRIC CONVERSION CHART

Liquid or Dry Measuring Cup
(based on an 8 ounce cup)
1/4 cup = 60 ml
1/3 cup = 80 ml
1/2 cup = 125 ml
3/4 cup = 190 ml
1 cup = 250 ml
2 cups = 500 ml

Liquid or Dry Measuring Cup
(based on a 10 ounce cup)
1/4 cup = 80 ml
1/3 cup = 100 ml
1/2 cup = 150 ml
3/4 cup = 230 ml
1 cup = 300 ml
2 cups = 600 ml

Liquid or Dry
Teaspoon and Tablespoon
1/4 tsp. = 1.5 ml
1/2 tsp. = 3 ml
1 tsp. = 5 ml
3 tsp. = 1 tbs. = 15 ml

Temperatures

°F		°C
200	=	100
250	=	120
275	=	140
300	=	150
325	=	160
350	=	180
375	=	190
400	=	200
425	=	220
450	=	230
475	=	240
500	=	260
550	=	280

Pan Sizes (1 inch = 25mm)
8-inch pan (round or square) = 200 mm x 200 mm
9-inch pan (round or square) = 225 mm x 225 mm
9 x 5 x 3-inch loaf pan = 225 mm x 125 mm x 75 mm
1/4 inch thickness = 5 mm
1/8 inch thickness = 2.5 mm

Pressure Cooker
100 Kpa = 15 pounds per square inch
70 Kpa = 10 pounds per square inch
35 Kpa = 5 pounds per square inch

Mass
1 ounce = 30 g
4 ounces = 1/4 pound = 125 g
8 ounces = 1/2 pounds = 250 g
16 ounces = 1 pound = 500 g
2 pounds = 1 kg

Key (America uses an 8 ounce cup — Britain uses a 10 ounce cup)

ml = milliliter
l = liter
g = gram
K = Kilo (one thousand)
mm = millimeter
m = mill (a thousandth)
°F = degrees Fahrenheit
°C = degrees Celsius
tsp. = teaspoon
tbs. = tablespoon
Kpa = (pounds pressure per square inch)
This configuration is used for pressure cookers only.

Metric equivalents are rounded to conform to existing metric measuring utensils.

SERVE CREATIVE, EASY, NUTRITIOUS MEALS WITH NITTY GRITTY® COOKBOOKS

Cappuccino/Espresso: The Book of Beverages
Recipes for the Pressure Cooker
The New Blender Book
The Well Dressed Potato
Convection Oven Cookery
The Steamer Cookbook
The Pasta Machine Cookbook
The Versatile Rice Cooker
The Dehydrator Cookbook
Waffles
The Coffee Book
The Bread Machine Cookbook
The Bread Machine Cookbook II
The Bread Machine Cookbook III
The Bread Machine Cookbook IV
The Sandwich Maker Cookbook
The Juicer Book
The Juicer Book II
Bread Baking (traditional), revised
The Kid's Cookbook
No Salt, No Sugar, No Fat Cookbook, revised
Cooking for 1 or 2, revised
Quick and Easy Pasta Recipes, revised
15-Minute Meals for 1 or 2
The 9x13 Pan Cookbook
Extra-Special Crockery Pot Recipes
Chocolate Cherry Tortes and Other Lowfat Delights
Low Fat American Favorites
Low Fat International Cuisine
Now That's Italian!
Fabulous Fiber Cookery
Low Salt, Low Sugar, Low Fat Desserts
Healthy Cooking on the Run, revised
Healthy Snacks for Kids
Muffins, Nut Breads and More
The Barbecue Book
The Wok
Quiche & Soufflé
New Ways to Enjoy Chicken
Favorite Seafood Recipes
New International Fondue Cookbook
Favorite Cookie Recipes
Authentic Mexican Cooking
Fisherman's Wharf Cookbook

Write or call for our free catalog.
BRISTOL PUBLISHING ENTERPRISES, INC.
P.O. Box 1737, San Leandro, CA 94577
(800) 346-4889; in California (510) 895-4461